Interesting facts

for curious minds

INDEX

Unexplored Stories

Reveals little-known events or hidden historical episodes

The Island of the Dolls: In Mexico, there is the Island of the Dolls, where a man placed dolls throughout the area in honor of a girl who drowned. It is said that the dolls are possessed.

The Dyatlov Pass Incident: In 1959, a group of Russian hikers died under mysterious circumstances in the Ural Mountains. Their tents were found torn, and some were partially clothed, leading to numerous theories.

The Solar Balloon Journey: In 1978, a hot air balloon named "Double Eagle II" successfully made the first non-stop transatlantic crossing, accomplishing an impressive feat.

The Underground City of Derinkuyu: In Turkey, an ancient underground city was discovered, believed to have been used as a refuge during invasions. It has multiple levels and can accommodate thousands of people.

The Mandela Effect: Some people recall historical events differently from reality, a phenomenon known as the "Mandela Effect," based on the mistaken belief that Nelson Mandela died in prison.

The Book of Kells: An illuminated manuscript from the 9th century, considered a masterpiece of Celtic art, that has survived the centuries and is housed in the Trinity College Library in Dublin.

The Mannahatta Project: Before becoming New York, the island of Manhattan was purchased by Dutch colonizers from Native Americans for goods valued at $24.

The D.B. Cooper Hijacking: In 1971, a man known as D.B. Cooper hijacked a plane, demanded a ransom, and then parachuted away, disappearing without a trace.

The Tunguska Explosion: In 1908, a massive explosion devastated trees in a remote area of Siberia. Although believed to be caused by a meteorite, no evidence of impact was found.

The Library of Alexandria: The ancient Library of Alexandria in Egypt was one of the greatest centers of knowledge in the ancient world. Unfortunately, it was destroyed under unknown circumstances, resulting in the loss of countless ancient texts.

Oak Island in Canada has been the setting for numerous unexplored stories and legends, including the mysterious disappearance of a group of fishermen in the 19th century.

There are still vast unexplored underwater areas, such as the Mariana Trench, where unique and unknown marine creatures have been discovered by science.

The Antarctic region is a sparsely explored location, and some expeditions have uncovered intriguing subglacial structures that raise questions about Earth's history.

In the 1980s, an uncontacted indigenous tribe was discovered in the Amazon jungle, highlighting the existence of unknown human communities in remote locations.

The Chernobyl Exclusion Zone, abandoned after the nuclear disaster, has given rise to unexplored stories of nature reclaiming the area and the possible presence of uncommon wildlife.

Son Doong Cave in Vietnam is the world's largest cave, discovered in 1991, but it was only fully explored in the last decade, unveiling a unique ecosystem and enormous passages.

The "Bennington Triangle" in Vermont, United States, has been the scene of unexplained disappearances and strange phenomena, sparking speculation about possible anomalies in the area.

Aokigahara Forest in Japan is known as the "suicide forest" and has been the subject of unexplored stories due to its dense atmosphere and the presence of abandoned personal belongings.

The recently discovered Lost City of Ciudad Blanca in Honduras, revealed using laser technology, has been a source of speculation and local legends for centuries.

The "fairy circles" in Namibia are circular formations of vegetation that have puzzled scientists for years, and their origin and function in the ecosystem are still not fully understood.

Geographical Mysteries

Bermuda Triangle: This area in the Atlantic Ocean has been famous for the unexplained disappearance of planes and ships over the years, generating numerous theories about its cause.

Carnac Stones: In France, alignments of megalithic stones in Carnac have puzzled archaeologists, as the exact reason for their arrangement remains unknown.

Nazca Lines: In Peru, extensive lines and geoglyphs in the desert have intrigued scientists and archaeologists, questioning the purpose behind these enormous figures traced on the land.

Mountains of the Moon: In Uganda, these mountains have been the backdrop for mysterious disappearances and sightings, giving rise to myths about unknown creatures.

Dragon's Triangle: Located in the South China Sea, this triangle has been associated with unexplained phenomena and ship disappearances.

13

Death Valley: In the United States, Death Valley is known for extreme temperatures and strange events, including reports of mysterious lights.

Easter Island: The moai statues on this South Pacific island are an archaeological enigma due to the way they were carved and transported, given the limited technology of the time.

The Dead Sea: Its high salinity allows people to easily float, and its unique composition has led to speculation about the existence of unknown creatures.

Tartary Strait: In the Sea of Japan, this strait has been the scene of ship disappearances and unexplained sightings.

Salar de Uyuni: In Bolivia, Salar de Uyuni is the world's largest salt flat. During the rainy season, it turns into a giant mirror reflecting the sky, creating a surreal landscape.

Bosnian Pyramids: In Bosnia, pyramids have been discovered that challenge conventional beliefs about the age and construction of such structures.

Iceland and Atlantis: Some theories suggest that Iceland could be part of the legendary Atlantis, given its unique geology and location in the North Atlantic. Bennington Triangle: In addition to disappearances, this triangle in Vermont has been linked to paranormal phenomena and sightings of unusual lights.

The Lost City of Iram: Known as "Iram of the Pillars" in Arabia, this lost city has been mentioned in Arabic literature and is believed to be hidden in the desert.

The Door to Hell: In Turkmenistan, a flaming gas crater has been burning for decades, creating a surreal and bewildering landscape.

The Devil's Triangle: In the North Sea, strange phenomena and disappearances have been reported, drawing comparisons to other mysterious triangles.

The Gates of Hell: In Uzbekistan, a massive flaming crater is known as "The Gates of Hell," created by a drilling accident.

Hoia-Baciu Forest: In Romania, this forest is famous for UFO sightings, paranormal activity, and the belief that it is haunted.

The Pacific Ring of Fire: This region is prone to earthquakes and volcanic activity, creating a ring of geological phenomena along the edge of the Pacific Ocean.

Death Valley in Russia: Not to be confused with its American namesake, this Russian valley is known for strange phenomena and a high incidence of disappearances.

Amazing Science

Unveil fascinating facts and astonishing scientific discoveries.

Point Nemo: It is the farthest point on the Earth's surface from any landmass and is located in the South Pacific. The International Space Station often disposes of its waste here.

The Placebo Effect: The positive response to a fake treatment demonstrates the power of the mind in recovery, and some studies suggest that even knowing one is taking a placebo can have benefits.

String Theory: In theoretical physics, string theory proposes that fundamental particles are not points but vibrating strings, aiming to unify quantum physics and general relativity.

Antimatter: It is the counterpart of normal matter, and when it encounters normal matter, they annihilate each other, releasing a large amount of energy. It is still a mystery why there is more matter than antimatter in the universe.

Quantum Holography: Some scientists suggest that our universe could be a holographic projection of data stored on the edges of space-time.

CRISPR-Cas9: This gene-editing tool allows scientists to precisely modify genes, offering revolutionary possibilities in medicine and biotechnology.

Photovoltaic Effect: Discovered in 1839, this phenomenon directly converts sunlight into electricity, forming the basis of solar technology.

Gödel's Theorem: In mathematics, this theorem demonstrated that there will always be statements that cannot be proven or disproven within a given logical system.

Heisenberg's Uncertainty Principle: This quantum principle states that the exact position and velocity of a subatomic particle cannot be known simultaneously.

Dark Matter: Although it constitutes approximately 27% of the universe, we cannot directly see it. Its presence is inferred by its gravitational influence on visible matter.

Paradox of Fermi: Despite the high probability of the existence of extraterrestrial life, we have not yet had contact with alien civilizations. The question is: Where are they?

Entropy of the Universe: According to the second law of thermodynamics, entropy, or disorder, always tends to increase, raising questions about the ultimate fate of the universe.

Doppler Effect: This phenomenon is observed when the frequency of a wave changes due to the relative motion between the wave source and the observer, and it applies to light, sound, and other waves.

Human Genome: Fully sequencing the human genome was a scientific milestone in 2003, allowing a deeper understanding of genetics and its role in health.

Exotic Matter: In particle physics, exotic matter is a form of matter that has properties opposite to normal matter, such as having negative density.

Paradox of Twins: According to the theory of relativity, twins who separate and travel at relativistic speeds will experience different aging, leading to this paradox.

Laws of Robotics: Proposed by Isaac Asimov, these ethical laws for artificial intelligence have influenced the discussion on the relationship between humans and machines.

Technological Singularity: Some futurists predict that artificial intelligence will eventually surpass human intelligence, leading to rapid social and technological change, known as the "singularity."

Butterfly Effect: In chaos theory, the butterfly effect suggests that small perturbations in a system can have significant and often unpredictable effects.

Neuroplasticity: The brain has the ability to reorganize and adapt continuously, even in adulthood, leading to neuroplasticity and opening new possibilities for rehabilitation and learning.

Unusual Cultures

Details traditions, rituals, and peculiar aspects of diverse cultures.

Matriarchy in Mosuo: In Mosuo culture in China, society is matriarchal, and property and decision-making pass from mother to daughter.

Apatani Tribe and Facial Decorations: In India, women of the Apatani tribe traditionally pierce their noses and wear large nose plugs and facial tattoos to appear less attractive and avoid being abducted.

Up Helly Aa Festival in the Shetland Islands: This celebration in Scotland involves residents dressing as Vikings, lighting torches, and burning a replica Viking ship.

Bride Kidnapping in Kyrgyzstan: In this tradition, a man kidnaps the woman he wishes to marry and then negotiates with her family to formalize the marriage.

Island of the Dolls in Mexico: In Xochimilco, there is an island covered with dolls hanging from trees, placed by a local resident to appease the spirit of a deceased girl.

Tribu Himba and Hair Care: In Namibia, the Himba apply a mixture of clay and fat to their bodies and hair, creating a distinctive appearance and protecting themselves from the sun.

Phuket Vegetarian Festival in Thailand: During this festival, participants abstain from eating meat and perform extreme rituals, including walking on hot coals and piercing their cheeks with sharp objects.

Ainu and Facial Tattoos: The Ainu culture in Japan has traditionally practiced facial tattooing, symbolizing the transition to adulthood and connection with the divine.

Mentawai People and Sikerei Ceremony: In Indonesia, the Mentawai perform a ceremony called Sikerei to mark the transition to adulthood, where men learn spiritual skills.

Thaipusam Festival in Malaysia: During this Hindu festival, devotees undergo body piercings and carry adorned structures to express their devotion and purification.

Tribu Surma and Lip Plates: In Ethiopia, women of the Surma tribe insert ceramic discs into their lower lips as part of a beauty tradition.

La Tomatina Festival in Spain: During this annual festival, participants throw tomatoes at each other in the streets of Buñol as a form of celebration.

Yaohnanen Ritual in Vanuatu: The Yaohnanen tribe believes in the divinity of Prince Philip of England and celebrates rituals in his honor.

Mail-Order Marriages in Mongolia: In some regions, mail-order marriages are practiced, allowing the betrothed to get to know each other through letters before the ceremony.

Sateré-Mawé Tribe and Initiation Rite: In Brazil, young individuals from this tribe participate in the "zum-zum" initiation rite, which involves wearing gloves filled with venomous ants for 10 minutes.

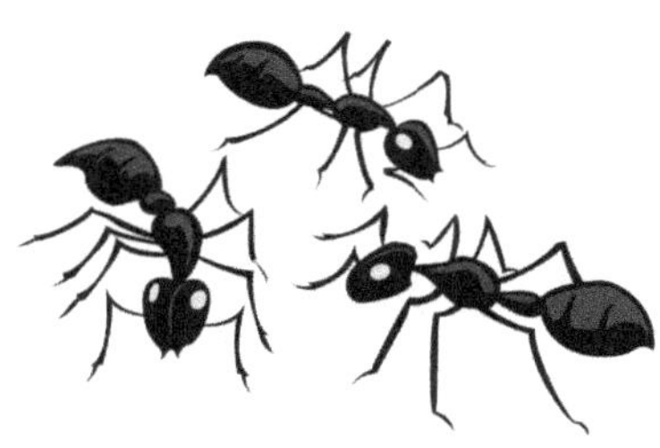

The Baining people and their Fire Festival: In Papua New Guinea, the Baining people celebrate the Fire Festival, where they light fires to rid themselves of the negative influences from the previous year.

Maasai Tribe and Vertical Jumping: The Maasai in Africa perform vertical jumps during ceremonies, showcasing bravery and physical strength.

Sardinian People and Giant's Tombs: In Sardinia, Italy, there are monumental tombs called "Giant's Tombs," constructed by the Nuragic culture.

Holi Festival in India: Known as the festival of colors, Holi involves throwing colored powders and water, celebrating the arrival of spring.

Sami People and their Relationship with Reindeer: The Sami community, located in Arctic areas of Norway, Sweden, Finland, and Russia, traditionally relies on reindeer herding for sustenance and has a deep connection with these animals.

Extraordinary Journeys

Tells anecdotes and curiosities of fascinating places around the world.

The Trans-Siberian Railway in Russia: With over 9,000 kilometers in length, it is the longest train route in the world, crossing eight time zones and offering a unique experience.

The International Date Line Crossing in Fiji: It is possible to be in two different days simultaneously when crossing this line in the Pacific Ocean.
The Silk Road: An ancient network of trade routes that connected Europe and Asia, playing a crucial role in cultural and commercial exchange.

The Mongol Rally in Mongolia: An adventure race challenging participants to cross Mongolia in small and unconventional vehicles.

The way to Santiago in Spain: A pilgrimage route leading to the city of Santiago de Compostela, traversing diverse landscapes and connecting people from around the world.

The Forbidden City in China: Situated in the heart of Beijing, it is a vast complex of palaces that served as the imperial residence for centuries.

The Underground City of Derinkuyu in Turkey: An ancient underground city built by the Hittites capable of accommodating thousands of people along with livestock and supplies.

The White City in Honduras: An urban legend describes a lost city in the Honduran jungle, whose ruins have not been fully uncovered.

The City of Petra in Jordan: Known as "the Rose City," Petra is famous for its rock-carved structures and its impressive entrance through the Al-Siq gorge.

Babylon in Iraq: With an ancient history, the ruins of Babylon house the famous Ishtar Gate and the Tower of Babel, according to biblical tradition.

Tokyo and Shibuya Crossing: The world's busiest pedestrian crossing is located in Shibuya, Tokyo, where thousands of people cross simultaneously during each traffic light change.

The City of the Dead in Cairo: A vast cemetery that has evolved to accommodate the living population, with buildings and services amid graves.

The Underground City of Coober Pedy in Australia: Due to high temperatures, many residents of Coober Pedy have built their homes underground.

Underwater City in Cuba: Off the coast of Cuba, there is an underwater city called "Cleopatra's City," with submerged ruins of an ancient settlement.

The City of Light, Varosha in Cyprus: An abandoned tourist city closed since 1974 due to political conflicts. The City of Statues in Easter Island: Over 900 stone-carved moai representing the ancestral culture of Rapa Nui.

Forbidden City in Beijing, China: A vast palace complex that served as the imperial residence for nearly 500 years and is now a major museum.

The Submerged City of Dwarka in India: Dwarka, mentioned in ancient texts as the city of the god Krishna, is believed to be submerged off the coast of India. Submarine explorations have revealed structures matching descriptions of the legendary city.

The Lost City of Heracleion in Egypt: Submerged in the Mediterranean Sea, Heracleion was a prosperous city that vanished over a thousand years ago. Archaeological discoveries include temples, statues, and artifacts that tell the story of this ancient metropolis.

City of Naples beneath the Ash Layer: The ancient Roman city of Pompeii was buried by ash and lava after the eruption of Mount Vesuvius in 79 AD. Centuries later, excavations revealed streets, buildings, and details of everyday life perfectly preserved under layers of ash and lava.

Incredible Animals

Showcases fascinating facts about fauna and astonishing behaviors.

The Chameleon and its Independent Eyes: The eyes of a chameleon can move independently, allowing them to monitor their environment more effectively and have a wide field of vision.

The Axolotl and Regeneration: This Mexican amphibian has the unique ability to regenerate parts of its body, including limbs, heart, and brain. It remains in a larval state throughout its life.

The Hummingbird, the Smallest Bird: Weighing less than 2 grams, hummingbirds are the smallest birds and can fly backward due to the special arrangement of their wings.

The Octopus and its Three Hearts: Octopuses have three hearts. Two pump blood to the gills, and the third pumps oxygenated blood to the rest of the body.

The Migration of Monarch Butterflies: Every year, millions of monarch butterflies travel thousands of kilometers from North America to Mexico to escape the winter cold.

The Elephant and its Memory: Elephants have an incredible long-term memory and can remember the location of water holes even after decades.

The Narwhal and its Giant Tusk: The narwhal's tusk, known as a horn, is actually a long tooth that can reach up to 3 meters in length.

The Hyena and its Unique Social Structure: Hyenas have a matriarchal social structure where females dominate over males, and their external genitalia resemble males.

The Mantis Shrimp and its Attack Speed: The mantis shrimp has one of the fastest claws in the animal kingdom, moving at a speed comparable to sound to catch prey.

The Okapi, Giraffe's Relative: Despite resembling a mix of zebra and giraffe, the okapi is the closest relative to giraffes and inhabits the forests of the Congo.

34

The Fruit Bat and its Ecological Importance: Fruit bats are key pollinators and contribute to seed dispersal in tropical ecosystems.

The Praying Mantis and Sexual Cannibalism: After mating, the female praying mantis occasionally devours the male, providing additional nutrients for egg production.

The Pistol Shrimp and its Explosive Sound: The pistol shrimp can generate a sound so powerful with its claws that it can break underwater bubbles and stun its prey.

The Bulldog Ant and its Painful Bite: Despite their small size, bulldog ants have a painful bite and can lock their jaws in position for extended periods.

The Giant Squid and its Enormous Eyes: Giant squids have the largest eyes in the animal kingdom, the size of a basketball, to detect prey in the dark depths of the ocean.

The Leaf-Nosed Bat and its Sophisticated Echolocation: These bats use leaf-shaped nasal structures to focus their echolocation signals, allowing them to accurately detect prey.

The Glass Frog and its Transparent Skin: Some glass frogs have transparent skin that allows their internal organs to be visible.

The Blue-Ringed Octopus and its Deadly Venom: Despite its small size, the blue-ringed octopus possesses one of the most potent venoms in the animal kingdom.

The 88 Butterfly in Malaysia: This butterfly has wings that resemble the number "88" when at rest, serving as camouflage against predators.

The Hermit Crab and its Shell Choices: Hermit crabs use abandoned shells to protect their soft bodies and move to larger shells as they grow.

Unusual Inventions

Examines strange creations and curiosities in the realm of inventiveness.

The Shoe Umbrella: Invented in the 1920s, it was an accessory designed to keep shoes dry during rain. The Shaving Machine Connected to a Lamp: Patented in 1928, this invention allowed for shaving while also having a light source.

The Windshield Hat: Designed in the 1930s, this hat had a plexiglass windshield to protect the face from the weather.

The Talking Dog Chair: A chair that, through a speaker, "speaks" on behalf of the dog, launched in the 1980s.

The Circular Bicycle: Invented in the 1930s, this circular-shaped bicycle allowed cyclists to see both forward and backward simultaneously.

The Bed Iron: An iron specially designed to smooth sheets while they are still on the bed, patented in the 1950s.

The Helicopter Umbrella: A combination of an umbrella and a helicopter, proposed as a way to fly in case of rain.

The All-Terrain Wheelchair: Equipped with tracks instead of wheels, this wheelchair was designed to move over rough terrain.

The Egg Toaster: A toaster that had space for toasting bread and cooking eggs simultaneously, popular in the 1950s.

Dog Sunglasses: Designed to protect dogs' eyes from the sun, especially useful for breeds prone to eye problems.

The Sprinkler Hat: A cap with a small built-in watering system, ideal for staying cool in warm climates.
The Selfie Stick with Fan: A selfie stick that includes a small fan to keep you cool while taking photos.

The Bird Hat for Cats: A bird-shaped hat placed on the head of cats, designed to entertain and photograph pets.

The Alarm Clock on Wheels: An alarm clock with wheels that moves around the room after ringing, forcing people to get up to turn it off.

The Musical Toothbrush: A toothbrush that plays music while you brush, encouraging a longer oral hygiene routine.

The Golf Ball Shaped Shaver: An invention that allowed shaving while simulating playing golf, providing additional entertainment.

The Soup Dispensing Belt: A belt with compartments to transport and dispense soup, a curious solution for eating on the go.

The Edible Keyboard: A keyboard made of chocolate that, according to its creators, was safe to use and savor.

The Smoker's Periscope: A device designed to allow smokers to peer over partitions while remaining in non-smoking areas.

The Zero Gravity Pen: A pen designed to write in zero gravity, developed for use in space missions.

NATURAL PHENOMENA
DESCRIBES UNIQUE AND UNCOMMON NATURAL EVENTS.

Polar Auroras: Auroras, also known as the Northern and Southern Lights, are produced by charged particles from the sun interacting with the Earth's atmosphere, creating stunning displays of colors.

Mirage: An optical phenomenon caused by the refraction of light, which can make distant objects appear in inaccessible locations, such as water in the middle of the desert.

Catatumbo Lightning: In Lake Maracaibo, Venezuela, the Catatumbo Lightning phenomenon occurs, a constant electrical spectacle due to the convergence of warm and cold winds.

Ozone Holes: Areas where the ozone layer has thinned, allowing harmful ultraviolet radiation to enter. The largest ozone hole is located over Antarctica.

Moving Rocks: In Death Valley, some heavy rocks move across the dry lake bed of Racetrack, leaving tracks in the ground. The exact phenomenon is not yet fully understood.

Light Pillars: Created by ice particles in the atmosphere, these luminous columns can extend vertically from Earth's light sources, such as streetlights.

Lenticular Cloud: A lens-shaped cloud that forms over mountains due to stable air flow.

Fire Tornadoes: Under extreme conditions, such as during wildfires, fire tornadoes can form, sucking in flames and generating dangerous winds.

Ball Lightning: A rare and poorly understood form of lightning, where a luminous energy ball forms and moves slowly through the air.

Fish Rain: A phenomenon where fish are transported by strong wind currents and fall from the sky, sometimes far from bodies of water.

Pink Snow: In some regions, snow can take on a pink hue due to the presence of algae containing red pigments.

Flowering Desert: In places like the Atacama Desert in Chile, after heavy rains, the desert can bloom with a wide variety of flowers.

Bioluminescent Waters: In certain locations, such as Mosquito Bay in Puerto Rico, water can light up with bright flashes due to bioluminescent microorganisms.

Supercells: Large rotating storms that can lead to tornadoes. They are known for their distinctive and long-lasting structure.

Southern Lights (Aurora Australis): Similar to the Northern Lights, but in the southern hemisphere. They can be observed in regions such as Antarctica and southern Australia.

Haboob Sandstorm: A massive and dense sandstorm that moves rapidly, common in desert regions.

Giant Hailstones: Occasionally, exceptionally large hailstones can fall during severe storms, causing significant damage.

Tsunamis: Generated by events like underwater earthquakes, tsunamis are giant waves that can flood coastal areas.

Blood Falls: In Antarctica, there are thermal springs containing iron-rich water, giving the appearance of water tinted red.

Geiser Fly: In Yellowstone National Park, thermophilic bacteria and minerals create vibrant colors around geysers, forming surreal landscapes.

Exotic Gastronomy

Explores surprising dishes and culinary practices from different cultures

Balut in the Philippines: A fertilized duck egg cooked and consumed with the partially developed embryo.

Sannakji in South Korea: A dish of live octopus cut into small pieces and served immediately.

Hakarl in Iceland: Fermented and decomposed shark, considered a local delicacy.

Escamoles in Mexico: Ant larvae collected from agave roots and considered a delicacy in Mexican cuisine. Casu Marzu in Italy: Pecorino cheese infested with maggot larvae that accelerate the fermentation process.

Takoyaki in Japan: Octopus-filled dough balls, cooked in a pan, and topped with sauces and bonito flakes.

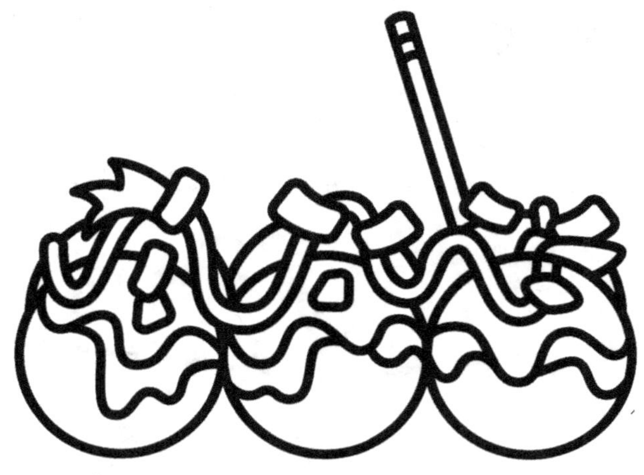

48

Huitlacoche in Mexico: An edible fungus that grows on corn, considered a delicacy in Mexican cuisine.

duck tongue in china: A dish that uses cooked duck tongue, which is then thinly sliced.

Khash in Armenia: A stew made with sheep's feet and head, often consumed as a comforting dish.

Surströmming in Sweden: Fermented herring stored in cans, known for its strong and distinctive smell.

Fugu in Japan: Blowfish containing deadly toxins. Only highly trained chefs can prepare it safely.

Mopane Worms in Africa: Caterpillar larvae of mopane moths, consumed as a snack in various African countries.

Criadillas in Spain: Testicles of bull or lamb cooked in various ways, considered delicacies in some regions.

Haggis in Scotland: A mixture of sheep's lungs, liver, and heart, combined with barley and spices, cooked in the stomach of the animal.

Cobra in Vietnam: Soup made with snake meat, considered aphrodisiac and consumed for its purported health benefits.

Tlayudas with Chapulines in Mexico: Giant tortillas covered with beans, cheese, and chapulines (grasshoppers).

Yacón Cheese Drink in Bolivia: A fermented beverage made from yacón cheese, an Andean root.

Civet Coffee in Indonesia: Coffee beans that have been ingested and excreted by civets, then collected, cleaned, and roasted to produce coffee.

Swallow's Nest Soup in China: A broth made with nests crafted from swallow's saliva, considered a luxurious delicacy.

Kangaroo in Australia: Kangaroo meat is consumed in Australia and is considered a more sustainable option than other red meats.

51

Inspiring Human Stories

Art with Feet: Without arms or hands, Tony Meléndez learned to play the guitar with his feet and became a talented musician and singer.

Overcoming in Sports: Terry Fox, diagnosed with bone cancer, embarked on a marathon to raise funds for cancer research, even after losing a leg.

Education Against All Odds: Malala Yousafzai, attacked by the Taliban for her advocacy of girls' education, became a global advocate and Nobel Peace Prize winner.

The Power of Forgiveness: Eva Kor, a Holocaust survivor and medical experiment victim at Auschwitz, forgave her captors and advocated for healing and reconciliation.

From Parking Lot to the NBA: Jeremy Lin, a basketball player with no offers from prominent universities, jumped from the developmental league to become a sensation in the NBA.

Breaking Barriers at NASA: Katherine Johnson, an African American mathematician, defied racial and gender discrimination at NASA, contributing to space missions.

The Power of Art in Prison: Jimmy Santiago Baca, incarcerated in his youth, learned to read and write in prison and became an acclaimed poet and advocate for education in prisons.

The Blind Runner: Without the ability to see, Marla Runyan competed in the Paralympic Games and later in the Olympic Games, excelling in track and field events.

Mountain Conqueror: Aron Ralston, trapped by a rock while climbing alone, amputated his own arm to free himself and survived in the desert.

Singer with Autism: Christopher Duffley, born blind and with autism, is a talented singer who has performed at events and on television programs.

Swimmer without Arms and Legs: Natalia Partyka, born without arms and with one leg shorter, competes in table tennis and swimming, participating in both the Paralympic and Olympic Games.

From Shoe Shiner to Billionaire: Howard Schultz, raised in poverty, worked as a shoe shiner before becoming the CEO of Starbucks and transforming the brand into a global giant.

Entrepreneurship in Old Age: Harland Sanders, known as Colonel Sanders, founded Kentucky Fried Chicken at the age of 65, turning it into a worldwide fast-food icon.

Paralympic Wheelchair Athlete: Tatyana McFadden, born with spina bifida, became a prominent Paralympic wheelchair athlete and won numerous gold medals.

Blind Writer: Helen Keller, deaf and blind since childhood, became a distinguished author and social advocate.

From Beggar to Philanthropist: Chris Gardner, homeless and a single father, overcame adversity to become a successful stockbroker and philanthropist.

Mountain Rescue: Armand du Plessis, who lost both legs in an accident, continued participating in extreme sports and undertaking mountain expeditions.

Gravity-Defying Dancer: Li Cunxin, raised in poverty in China, became one of the leading dancers of the Houston Ballet after a transformative experience.

Bullying Fighter: Lizzie Velasquez, born with a rare condition affecting her appearance, became an anti-bullying advocate and motivational speaker.

Triumph over Multiple Sclerosis: Montel Williams, diagnosed with multiple sclerosis, became a successful television host and advocate for awareness about the disease.

Famous Figures

Surprising facts about their lives

Jim Carrey's Career Change: Before becoming famous, Jim Carrey worked as a janitor at a factory and as a security guard. He decided to pursue his dream of becoming a comedian after his family faced financial difficulties.

Madonna's Failed Audition: In her first audition for a band, Madonna played the bongos and was rejected for being "too annoying." She later became one of the most influential artists in the history of pop music.

Morgan Freeman's Late Breakthrough: Despite his impressive career, Morgan Freeman didn't land his first major film role until the age of 50 when he portrayed Hoke Colburn in "Driving Miss Daisy."

Gal Gadot's Military Past: Before portraying Wonder Woman, Gal Gadot served in the Israel Defense Forces as a physical combat instructor.

Bill Murray's Doppelganger: Bill Murray has a look-alike named Tom Hanks. Both actors have joked about their physical resemblance over the years.

Oprah Winfrey's First Job: Before becoming the "Queen of Media," Oprah Winfrey started her career as a news announcer on the radio at the age of 19.

James Cameron's Invention: Before directing successful films like "Titanic" and "Avatar," James Cameron worked as a truck driver. It was during a period of unemployment that he wrote the script for "The Terminator."

Quentin Tarantino's Past: Quentin Tarantino worked as a video store clerk before becoming an acclaimed film director. During his time at the store, he self-educated on movies and cinema.

Robin Williams' Stand-up Beginnings: Robin Williams began his career as a stand-up comedian in San Francisco, where he was discovered for the TV show "Happy Days."

Brad Pitt's Stint in Advertising: Before achieving fame in Hollywood, Brad Pitt worked at a refrigerator delivery company and appeared in television commercials for Levi's.

Barack Obama's Job at Baskin-Robbins: Antes de convertirse en el 44° presidente de los Estados Unidos, Barack Obama tuvo un trabajo de verano sirviendo helado en una tienda Baskin-Robbins.

Steve Jobs's Affection for Meditation: Steve Jobs, el cofundador de Apple, practicó la meditación zen durante su vida y atribuyó parte de su éxito y creatividad a esta disciplina.

Tom Ford's Career in Fashion: Before directing films and creating his own fashion line, Tom Ford worked as a fashion designer for renowned brands such as Gucci and Yves Saint Laurent.

Chris Pratt's Past: Before becoming a movie star, Chris Pratt worked as a street coupon salesman and as a stripper at bachelor parties.

Natalie Portman's College Life: A pesar de su éxito como actriz, Natalie Portman obtuvo un título en Psicología de la Universidad de Harvard mientras trabajaba en películas exitosas como "Star Wars: Episode I – The Phantom Menace".

Mayim Bialik's Scientific Inclination: Antes de interpretar a Amy Farrah Fowler en "The Big Bang Theory", Mayim Bialik obtuvo un doctorado en Neurociencia.

Ellen DeGeneres's Comedy Beginnings: Ellen DeGeneres comenzó su carrera de comediante actuando en pequeños clubes de comedia en Nueva Orleans antes de su ascenso a la fama.

Adele's Stage Fright: La talentosa cantante Adele sufre de miedo escénico y, en varias ocasiones, ha admitido sentir ansiedad antes de sus actuaciones.

J.K. Rowling's Tale of Triumph: Before penning the successful *Harry Potter* book series, J.K. Rowling was a single mother living on welfare. Her initial manuscript faced rejections from multiple publishers before securing the publication that would change her life.

Steven Spielberg's First Job: Before becoming an iconic director, Steven Spielberg was hired by Universal Studios as an unpaid intern. During that period, he created a short film that eventually landed him his first seven-year contract with the studio.

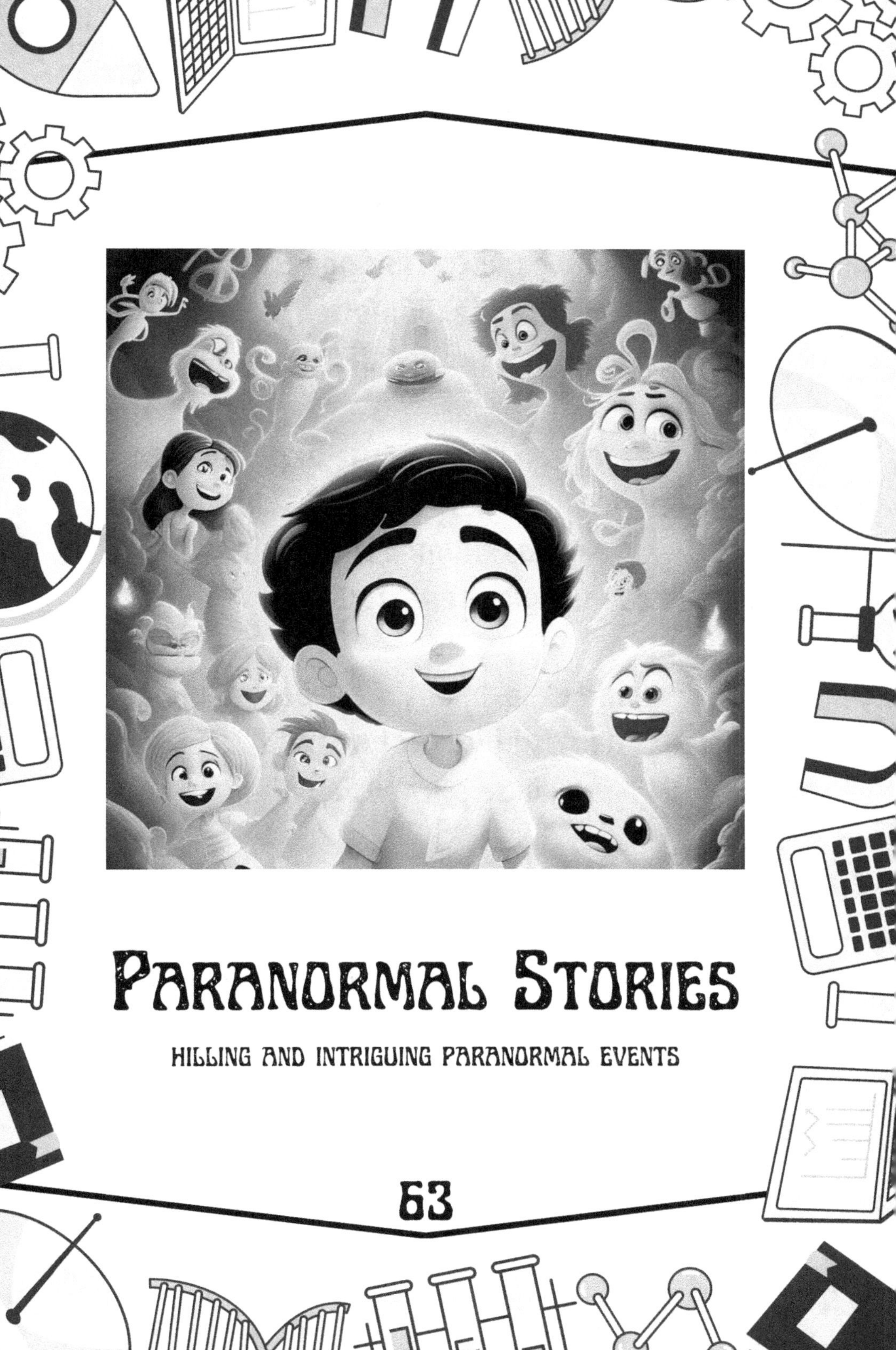

PARANORMAL STORIES

HILLING AND INTRIGUING PARANORMAL EVENTS

The Amityville House: The house in Amityville, New York, was the setting for alleged paranormal events that inspired horror books and movies.

Crop Circles: Complex patterns appearing in crop fields without apparent explanation, often associated with paranormal theories and UFOs.

Enfield Poltergeist: A famous case of poltergeist activity that occurred in the 1970s in Enfield, England, where it was claimed that a girl was possessed by malevolent entities.

The Philadelphia Experiment: A purported military experiment on invisibility that was said to have taken place in 1943 but whose authenticity is questioned.

Hessdalen Lights Phenomenon: In Norway, this phenomenon involves mysterious lights appearing in the sky, often with varied shapes and colors. These lights have been observed since the 1930s, and despite numerous studies, scientists have not reached a conclusive explanation about their origin.

The Legend of La Llorona: A popular Latin American tale about a woman who weeps for the loss of her children and is believed to appear as a ghost.

The Stanley Hotel and The Shining: The Stanley Hotel in Colorado, known for its paranormal activity, inspired Stephen King's novel "The Shining."

Encounters with Men in Black: Reports of encounters with figures dressed in black who investigate UFO sightings and paranormal phenomena, sometimes in an intimidating manner.

The Exorcism of Robbie Mannheim: The case that inspired the movie "The Exorcist," involving a boy known as Robbie who was allegedly possessed by a demon.

The Loch Ness Monster: Legends about an aquatic monster in Loch Ness, Scotland, although there is no conclusive evidence of its existence.

The Montauk Project: A series of conspiracy theories suggesting paranormal experiments and time travel at the Montauk military base in Long Island.

The Lady in White: Legends of a spectral figure dressed in white that appears in various cultures and is believed to be connected to tragic events.

Apparitions in Old Photos: Old photographs often show alleged ghostly apparitions or unexplained figures.

The Gray Man of Pawleys Island: A local legend telling the story of a gray-clad man from a bygone era who appears before major storms on Pawleys Island.

The Curse of King Tutankhamun: It is said that those who were involved in the opening of the tomb of Pharaoh Tutankhamun suffered misfortunes or mysterious deaths.

Astral Travel: Experiences in which consciousness is believed to separate from the physical body and travel to other dimensions.

The Island of the Dolls: In Mexico, the Island of the Dolls is filled with dolls hanging from trees, believed to be possessed by spirits.

The Man Who Vanished from Time Square: In 1950, Rudolph Fentz supposedly appeared in Time Square, New York, suddenly from 1876, but then vanished again.

Salem Witch Trials: The witch trials in Salem, Massachusetts, in the 17th century left a dark mark on history and persist in paranormal stories.

The Marfa Lights: Unexplained lights that appear in the Marfa desert, Texas, and have baffled observers for decades.

DINOSAURS

Interesting discoveries and observations

Feathers in Dinosaurs: Evidence has been found that some dinosaurs, such as the Velociraptor, had feathers, suggesting that not all were scaly reptiles.

T-Rex with Small Arms: Although the Tyrannosaurus Rex (T-Rex) had powerful jaws, its arms were small and not very functional compared to the size of its body.

Flying Dinosaurs: Pterosaurs, like the Pteranodon, were flying reptiles, not dinosaurs, despite often being associated with them.

Aquatic Dinosaurs: Some dinosaurs, like the Spinosaurus, were semiaquatic and spent a significant amount of their time in the water.

Dinosaurs Smaller than a Chicken: The Microraptor, a small feathered dinosaur, was approximately the size of a crow and much smaller than most popular depictions of dinosaurs.

Mass Extinction: Dinosaurs fell victim to a mass extinction event that occurred at the end of the Cretaceous period, approximately 65 million years ago. An asteroid or comet impact is believed to have contributed to this event.

The Largest Dinosaur: The Argentinosaurus is one of the largest known dinosaurs, with an estimated length of up to 100 feet (30 meters) and a weight of around 100 tons.

Feathered Carnivorous Dinosaurs: Some carnivorous dinosaurs, such as the Dilophosaurus, have been found to have feathers, challenging the traditional image of dinosaurs with scaly skin.

Dinosaur Footprints: Numerous fossilized dinosaur trackways exist, some of which show evidence of social and migratory behaviors.

Brachiosaurus' Long Neck: The Brachiosaurus had an extremely long neck, enabling it to reach vegetation at the tops of trees.

Carnotaurus' Small Teeth: The Carnotaurus had very small teeth compared to its body size, but it compensated by using a powerful jaw.

Dinosaur with Nasal Horns: The Styracosaurus had a series of horns on its head, including a distinctive one on its nose, resembling a rhinoceros.

Largest Dinosaur Egg: The Macroelongatoolithus, a type of dinosaur egg, is the largest known, with diameters exceeding 13 inches (33 cm).

Dinosaurs with Crests: Many dinosaurs, like the Parasaurolophus, had crests on their heads, possibly used for making sounds and communication.

Dinosaur with Bony Plates: The Stegosaurus had bony plates along its back, and the exact function of these plates is still not fully understood.

Not So Big Velociraptor: Unlike its portrayal in "Jurassic Park," the Velociraptor was quite small, approximately the size of a turkey.

Bipedal and Quadrupedal Dinosaurs: Some dinosaurs walked on two legs (bipedal), while others, like the Triceratops, were quadrupedal.

Flying Dinosaurs: Modern birds are considered descendants of dinosaurs, specifically feathered theropods like the Archaeopteryx.

Marine Dinosaurs: Plesiosaurs and ichthyosaurs were not dinosaurs, but they shared the dinosaur era and were marine reptiles.

Fossils with Soft Tissues: In some exceptional cases, soft tissues of dinosaurs, such as feathers and skin, have been preserved, providing unique information about their physical appearance.

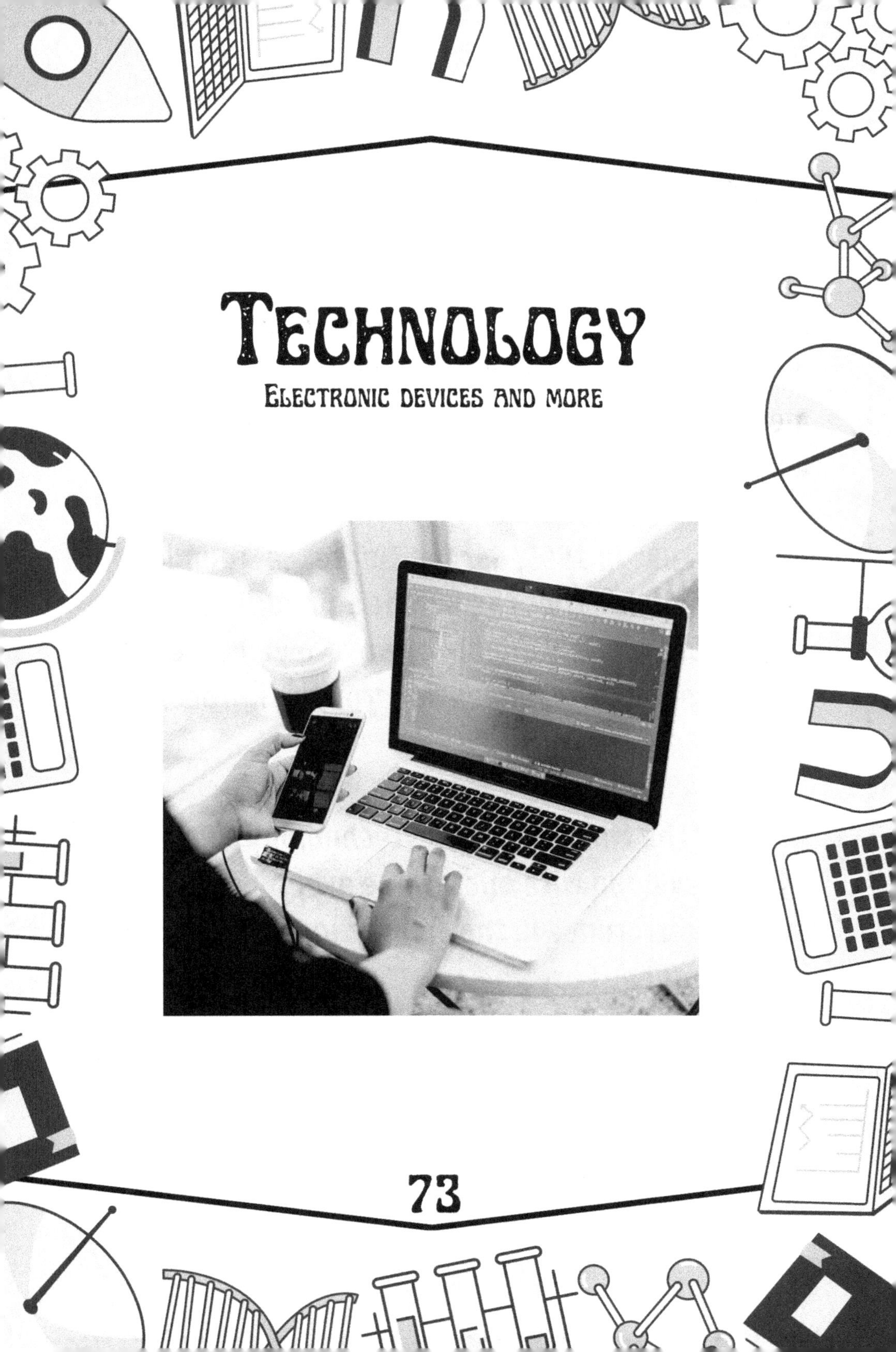

TECHNOLOGY

ELECTRONIC DEVICES AND MORE

First Electronic Computer: The ENIAC, the first general-purpose electronic computer, occupied an area of 167 square meters and weighed around 30 tons.

First Mobile Phone: The first commercial mobile phone, the Motorola DynaTAC 8000X, released in 1983, measured about 30 centimeters in height and weighed almost a kilogram.

Moore's Law: In 1965, Gordon Moore, co-founder of Intel, predicted that the number of transistors on a chip would roughly double every two years, setting a guideline for the exponential growth of processing power.

WiFi and the Microwave: WiFi technology shares a frequency band with microwave ovens, which can cause interference in the connection when both are in simultaneous use.

The First Emoji: The first emoji was created in 1999 by Shigetaka Kurita in Japan, and it represented a heart.

74

The First Video Game: "Pong" was the first commercially successful video game and was released by Atari in 1972. It involved a virtual simulation of ping-pong.

Python Programming Language: Python, a high-level programming language, is named after Monty Python, a British comedy group.

GPS and General Relativity: Satellites in the Global Positioning System (GPS) must adjust their clocks to account for time dilation predicted by Einstein's theory of general relativity.

Bits and Bytes Terminology: The term "bit" comes from the combination of "binary" and "digit," while "byte" was coined by Werner Buchholz in 1956 and represents a sequence of 8 bits.

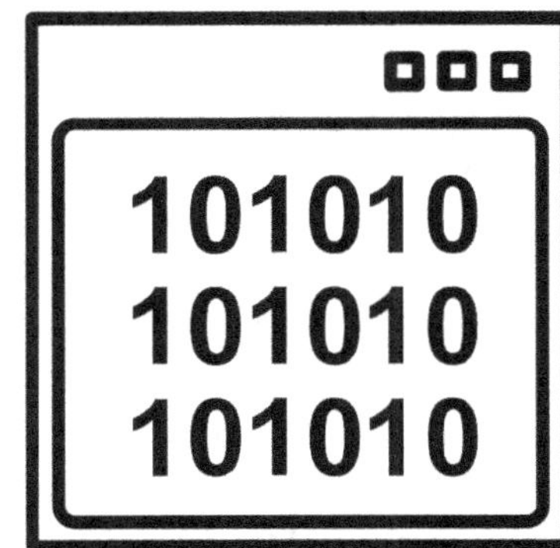

75

The First Website: The first website was created by Tim Berners-Lee and went online in 1991. It described the World Wide Web project and provided information on how to create web pages.

The First Mouse: Douglas Engelbart invented the first mouse in 1964. It was made of wood and had two perpendicular wheels that moved in two directions.

Origin of the Bluetooth Name: The name Bluetooth comes from the Danish king Harald "Bluetooth" Gormsson, famous for unifying Danish tribes. Bluetooth technology aims to unify electronic devices through wireless connection.

QR Code and Toyota: The QR code (Quick Response) was invented by Masahiro Hara, an engineer at Toyota, to track parts in automobile manufacturing.

The First Digital Camera: The first commercial digital camera, the Dycam Model 1, was released in 1990 and had a resolution of 320x240 pi

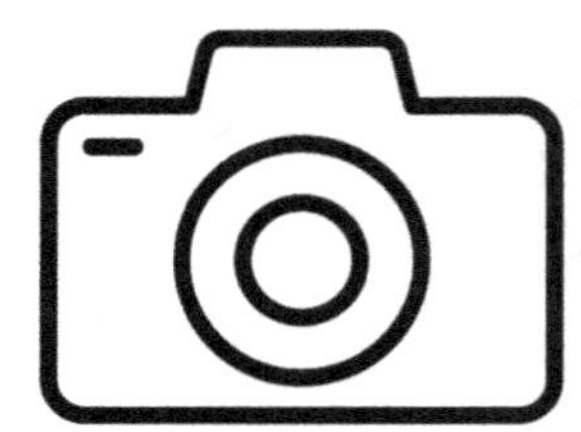

The First Hard Drive: The IBM 305 RAMAC, released in 1956, was the first hard drive and weighed around a ton. It had a storage capacity of 5 megabytes.

GIF and CompuServe: The GIF image format was created by Steve Wilhite in 1987 while working for CompuServe.

The First Email: The first email was sent by Ray Tomlinson in 1971. It contained the text line "QWERTYUIOP."

The First 3D Printer: Chuck Hull invented the first 3D printer in 1983 and named it "stereolithography."

Amazon and Books: When Jeff Bezos founded Amazon in 1994, it initially only sold books. The idea of expanding to other products developed later.

Barcode and Chewing Gum: The invention of the barcode was inspired by Joseph Woodland's Morse code reading on the beach. He was thinking of an efficient way to automate data reading in supermarkets while chewing gum.

Curiosities about Cinema

Let's talk about movies

The Longest Movie: "Logistics," an unusual experimental film, has a duration of over 35 days and was first screened in 2012.

The Shortest Movie: "Fresh Guacamole" has a duration of only 1 minute and 40 seconds and is the shortest film ever nominated for an Academy Award.

Box Office Record: James Cameron's "Avatar" is the highest-grossing film in history, surpassing 2.8 billion dollars in revenue.

The First Blockbuster: Steven Spielberg's "Jaws," released in 1975, is considered the first blockbuster film, changing the way movies were promoted and distributed.

Movie with Most Oscar Wins: "Ben-Hur" (1959), "Titanic" (1997), and "The Lord of the Rings: The Return of the King" (2003) share the record for winning 11 Oscars each.

The Youngest Oscar Winner: Tatum O'Neal won the Academy Award for Best Supporting Actress for "Paper Moon" (1973) at the age of 10, making her the youngest winner in the history of the Academy Awards.

The First Animated Feature Film: "Snow White and the Seven Dwarfs" (Blancanieves y los siete enanitos), released by Disney in 1937, was the first full-length animated feature film.

Most Filmed Character: Bram Stoker's "Dracula" is the literary character that has appeared in the most films, surpassing 200 cinematic adaptations.

The First Sound in Cinema: "The Jazz Singer" (1927) was the first film to incorporate spoken dialogue and synchronized music, marking the beginning of the era of sound in cinema.

Movie with the Most Explosions: "Hot Shots! Part Deux" (1993) holds the record for the film with the most explosions, with a total of 460.

Most Expensive Film in History: "Pirates of the Caribbean: On Stranger Tides" (2011) is the most expensive film ever made, with a budget of around $378.5 million.

The Film Most Accidentally Recorded: In 1969, a British company confused the film "The Lion in Winter" with an erotic production titled "The Lion in Winter" and mistakenly screened the wrong movie in several theaters.

The Fastest-Filmed Movie: "Russian Ark" (2002) is a Russian film shot in a single continuous take, making it one of the longest-ever films, with a duration of 96 minutes.

The First Kiss in Cinema: The first kiss in a movie was shown in "The Kiss" (1896), a short film directed by William Heise.

The First Sound Western: "The Big Trail" (1930), directed by Raoul Walsh, was the first sound western film.

The Film with the Most Explosions in a Sequence: "The Lord of the Rings: The Two Towers" (2002) features a 20-minute sequence with 150,000 virtual explosions.

The Most Edited Film: The movie "Koyaanisqatsi" (1982) has only 20 cuts in its 87-minute duration, making it one of the least edited films.

Most Awarded Film at Cannes: Quentin Tarantino's "Pulp Fiction" (1994) won the Palme d'Or at the Cannes Film Festival and became a cultural phenomenon.

Film with the Most Visual Effects: "Avengers: Endgame" (2019) has over 3,000 shots with visual effects, setting a record in this aspect.

The Longest Projected Film: "The Longest Most Meaningless Movie in the World" (1970) has a duration of 48 hours and was screened in its entirety once.

Mysteries of Outer Space

Explores cosmic phenomena, black holes, and mysteries of the universe

Supermassive Black Holes: At the center of many galaxies, including the Milky Way, there is a supermassive black hole that can be millions or even billions of times more massive than our Sun.

Einstein's Theory of Relativity: Einstein's general theory of relativity predicts the existence of wormholes, hypothetical tunnels in spacetime that could connect different regions of the universe.

Cosmic Microwave Background Radiation: Cosmic microwave background radiation is a faint microwave radiation that fills the universe and is a remnant of the Big Bang, providing a window into the early stages of the cosmos.

Expansion of the Universe: The universe is constantly expanding, a discovery that led to the formulation of the Big Bang theory.

Dark Matter: Approximately 27% of the universe is composed of dark matter, an invisible substance that does not interact with light but whose presence is revealed by its gravitational effects.

Fermi Paradox: Despite the vastness of the universe, the Fermi Paradox raises the question of why we haven't detected signals from extraterrestrial life, given the many possible civilizations in the cosmos.

Supernovae and Heavy Elements: Supernovae, massive stellar explosions, are responsible for the creation of elements heavier than iron, such as gold and platinum.

Quasars: Quasars are extremely bright and distant astronomical objects, powered by supermassive black holes at the centers of galaxies.

Gravitational Waves: Gravitational waves are ripples in spacetime caused by violent cosmic events, such as black hole mergers or neutron star collisions.

Exoplanets: Thousands of exoplanets outside our solar system have been discovered, some of which may have conditions conducive to life.

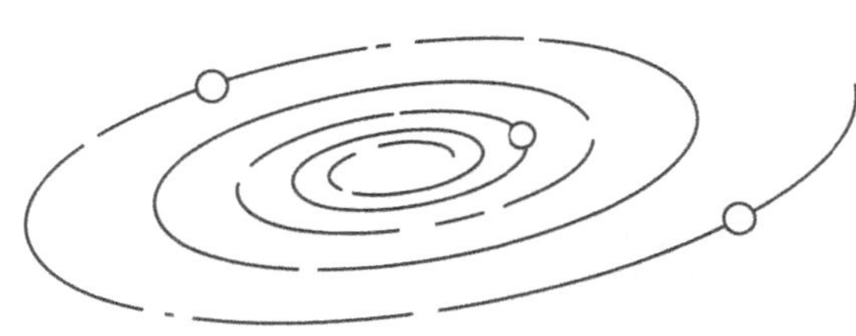

Interstellar Travel: The Voyager 1 spacecraft is the farthest human-made object from Earth and has entered interstellar space.

Magnetars: Magnetars are neutron stars with extremely powerful magnetic fields, capable of generating gamma-ray bursts that surpass in intensity any other known source.

Nebulas: Nebulas are vast clouds of gas and dust in space, some of which are stellar nurseries where new stars are born.

The Great Attractor: The Great Attractor is a mysterious concentration of mass that exerts a significant gravitational force in our region of the universe, affecting the motion of nearby galaxies.

Antimatter: Antimatter is a form of matter composed of antiparticles, and its existence is confirmed through experiments in laboratories and cosmic observations.

Kuiper Belt: Beyond Neptune's orbit, the Kuiper Belt hosts numerous icy objects, including Pluto, and is a key region for studying the outer solar system.

Water on Other Planets: Signs of water have been discovered on various planets and moons outside of Earth, increasing the possibility of finding life within our solar system.

Cosmic Catastrophes: Events such as neutron star collisions and supernovas can have dramatic consequences on the structure and evolution of the universe.

Water in Interstellar Space: Water has been detected in molecular clouds in interstellar space, suggesting that this life-sustaining liquid might be more common than previously thought.

The Big Freeze: In the distant future, the universe is predicted to experience the "Big Freeze" as it expands and stars burn out, leaving a cold and dark cosmos.

World's Smartest Individuals

Historical figures remembered for their great abilities

Albert Einstein and His Brain: After Einstein's death in 1955, his brain was preserved for scientific study, though the results of such studies remain debated.

Stephen Hawking and the "Game of Life": Hawking enjoyed the "Game of Life," a cellular automaton, and contributed to the development of its rules.

Marilyn vos Savant and her IQ: Marilyn vos Savant, considered the person with the highest recorded IQ, was included in the Guinness World Records for her score.

Leonardo da Vinci and Dyslexia: It is believed that Leonardo da Vinci, one of history's greatest geniuses, may have had dyslexia, a condition that did not hinder his remarkable contributions.

Garry Kasparov and Artificial Intelligence: Garry Kasparov, world chess champion, lost to IBM's Deep Blue supercomputer in 1997, marking a milestone in the relationship between humans and artificial intelligence.

Terence Tao and Gold Medals: Terence Tao, a mathematical prodigy, won a gold medal at the International Mathematical Olympiad at the age of 13.

Marie Curie and her Two Nobel Prizes: Marie Curie is the only person in history to receive Nobel Prizes in two different scientific fields: physics and chemistry.

Nikola Tesla and Hypersensitivity: Tesla was known for having hypersensitivity to light and sound, allowing him to perceive details that others couldn't.

James Woods and his High IQ: Actor James Woods has a very high IQ and attended the Massachusetts Institute of Technology (MIT) before pursuing acting.

Marissa Mayer and Google: Marissa Mayer, former Vice President of Google, had an exceptional IQ and played a key role in the development of products like Google Search.

Richard Feynman and Musical Skill: Feynman, a theoretical physicist, was also an accomplished bongo player and enjoyed Latin music.

Ruth Lawrence and the University of Oxford: Ruth Lawrence, a mathematical prodigy, entered the University of Oxford at the age of 12.

William James Sidis and Hypercognition: William James Sidis, considered one of the most intelligent individuals, had an exceptional learning ability and is credited with an extremely high IQ.

Shakuntala Devi and Mental Calculation: Shakuntala Devi, known as the "Human Computer," demonstrated astonishing mathematical abilities, including mentally solving complex problems.

John von Neumann and Polymathy: Von Neumann, a mathematician and physicist, excelled in multiple fields, from game theory to computer science and quantum physics.

Judit Polgár and Chess: Judit Polgár, considered the greatest female chess player of all time, defeated several male world champions.

Christopher Langan and the "Smartest Man": Christopher Langan is known as the "smartest man" due to his high IQ, although his story is complex.

URBAN LEGENDS

UNCOVER STORIES AND URBAN MYTHS THAT HAVE CAPTURED POPULAR IMAGINATION

The White Lady: This urban legend tells the story of a woman dressed in white who appears in lonely places or on roads, often associated with tragic events.

The Boogeyman: An urban myth that scares children, this character is said to kidnap naughty kids.

La Llorona: A figure present in many Latin American cultures, La Llorona is a weeping woman mourning her lost children, and her cry is said to be heard near bodies of water.

The Ghost Hitchhiker: Stories of travelers picking up hitchhikers only to discover that they mysteriously vanish during the journey.

The Cemetery Bride: It is said that a deceased bride returns to seek revenge or to reconcile with her lost love.

94

The Hook on the Car Door: The warning about a serial killer using a hook to attack couples in parked cars in secluded places.

Bloody Mary: The legend of invoking a sinister figure called Bloody Mary by staring into a mirror and repeating her name three times.

Momo: A terrifying figure that supposedly sends threatening and violent messages through instant messaging apps, especially targeting children.

The Hairy Hand: A story involving a hairy and monstrous creature that appears on people's beds at night.

The Ouija Board Game: It is believed that playing with a Ouija board can open doors to the paranormal, and spirits can communicate through it.

The Lantern Serial Killer: A serial killer who stalks in dark places, holding a lantern to find his victims.

The City of Cats: A legend suggesting that there is a secret city populated only by cats, hidden in some remote location.

The Stream Sack Man: A character said to live in sewer systems and come out at night to catch disobedient children.

The Macabre Musical Chairs Game: A macabre variant of the musical chairs game, where the loser faces supernatural consequences.

The Organ Sack Man: A legend warning about a man who steals organs from unsuspecting people.

El Chupacabras: A myth that originated in Latin America, describing a creature that sucks the blood of domestic animals.

The Popcorn Kid: A story that warns about a child who died from eating popcorn that exploded in his stomach.

The Internet Sack Man: A modern legend warning about hidden dangers on the internet and advising children on online behavior.

The Bag Man: Similar to the Boogeyman, this figure is said to carry naughty children inside his bag.

The Infinite Mirror Game: A game that involves looking at oneself in a mirror in complete darkness, with the belief that supernatural things can be seen.

Fascinating Historical Figures

Learn curious and lesser-known details about prominent historical figures

Leonardo da Vinci and mirror writing: Leonardo da Vinci often wrote in mirror, from right to left, meaning his writings could only be read correctly in a mirror.

Albert Einstein and his laceless shoes: Einstein opted for laceless shoes, claiming it was a waste of time to tie them.

Winston Churchill and his habit of working in bed: Churchill had the habit of working in bed until noon, claiming it allowed him to rest and work at the same time.

Cleopatra and her donkey milk baths: The famous Queen Cleopatra was known for her beauty rituals, including baths with donkey milk to keep her skin soft and radiant.

Napoleon Bonaparte and his fear of cats: Despite conquering much of Europe, Napoleon had a significant fear of cats.

Benjamin Franklin and his love for air baths: Franklin took "air baths" daily, sitting naked in front of an open window.

Marie Curie and her radioactive notes: The notebooks and personal belongings of Marie Curie, a pioneer in radiation research, are still highly radioactive and require protection.

Isaac Newton and his dog Diamond: Newton had a dog named Diamond, who accidentally destroyed years of work by knocking over an inkwell onto his writings.

Gandhi and his peculiar diet: Mahatma Gandhi was a vegetarian and followed a diet that included fruits, nuts, milk, and honey.

Catherine the Great and her collection of erotic art: The Russian Empress Catherine the Great had an extensive collection of erotic art that remains private to this day.

Abraham Lincoln and his axe-throwing skill: Lincoln was an expert at throwing axes and participated in competitions in his youth.

Mozart and his fascination with cats: Mozart composed a piece called "Kätzchen Menuett" (Kitten Minuet), inspired by his love for cats.

Elizabeth I and her lead-based makeup: Queen Elizabeth I of England used makeup that contained lead, which eventually contributed to her deteriorating health.

Nikola Tesla and his obsession with pigeons: Tesla had a deep connection with pigeons and even claimed that a white pigeon had visited him to announce the death of his mother.

Joan of Arc and her ability to foresee the future: Joan of Arc claimed to have visions that allowed her to foresee the future and guide her troops.

101

Frida Kahlo and her love for exotic animals: Frida Kahlo had several exotic animals such as monkeys, deer, and an eagle.

Genghis Khan and his fear of writing: Despite his conquests, Genghis Khan never learned to read and write.

Christopher Columbus and his belief in the existence of mermaids: Columbus noted in his journal that he had seen mermaids during his voyage to the New World, although they were likely manatees.

George Washington and his ivory teeth: Contrary to legend, George Washington's teeth were not made of wood but carved from animal and human ivory.

Tutankhamun and his golf club: Remains of an ancient golf club were found in Tutankhamun's tomb, suggesting that the game might have existed much earlier than previously thought.

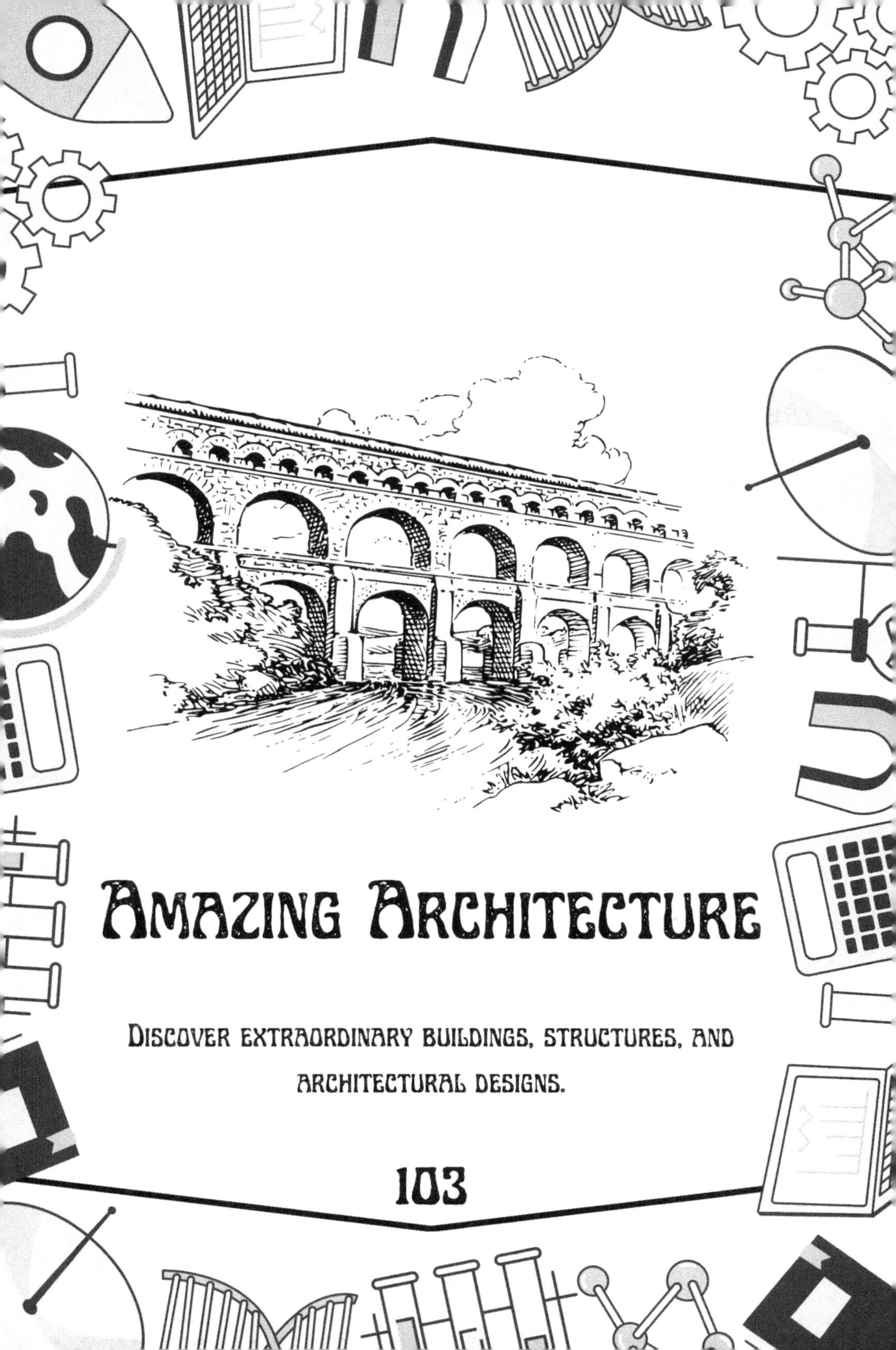

Amazing Architecture

Discover extraordinary buildings, structures, and architectural designs.

103

The Parthenon and its inclined columns: To counteract optical illusion and create a straight appearance, the columns of the Parthenon in Athens are slightly inclined inwards.

Neuschwanstein Castle and its inspiration for Disney: Neuschwanstein Castle in Bavaria, Germany, inspired the design of Disney castles, including the famous company logo.

The House of Shells and its embedded shells: In Salamanca, Spain, the House of Shells has over 300 shells embedded in its façade, symbolizing the Order of the Shell of Santiago.

The stairs of the Palace of Santa Catalina: In Potosí, Bolivia, the Palace of Santa Catalina has stairs that spiral counterclockwise, designed to give defenders an advantage in case of a surprise attack.

The Rialto Bridge and its innovative design: The Rialto Bridge in Venice, Italy, was the first bridge built over the Grand Canal and is known for its unique arch design.

Hallgrímskirkja Church and its nature-inspired design: In Reykjavik, Iceland, Hallgrímskirkja Church has architecture that mimics the shape of basalt columns found in Icelandic nature.

Brasília Cathedral and its futuristic appearance: Designed by Oscar Niemeyer, Brasília Cathedral in Brazil looks more like a spaceship than a traditional religious building.

Chain Bridge and the story of the lion of Budapest: The Chain Bridge in Budapest, Hungary, has two lion statues at each end, and legend has it that if the lions roar, the river will overflow.

The Butterfly House: Located in Santiago, Chile, this house has a façade decorated with 540 butterflies made of copper, representing transformation and renewal.

Pyramid of Cestius and its connection to ancient Rome: In Rome, Italy, the Pyramid of Cestius, built in 12 B.C., is a rare example of Egyptian architecture in the city.

The Malva House and its upside-down windows: In Vienna, Austria, the Malva House features windows that appear to be upside down, designed to challenge the monotony of the surrounding architecture.

The Batalha Monastery and its inverted rose window: In Portugal, the Batalha Monastery has an inverted rose window representing a fallen angel, an unusual detail in religious architecture.

The Kailasa Temple and its monumental excavation: The Kailasa Temple in Ellora, India, is a monolithic structure excavated from rock, carved vertically from top to bottom.

The Palau de la Música Catalana and its stunning stained glass: In Barcelona, Spain, this palace boasts an impressive stained glass forming a sun, designed to naturally illuminate the interior.

The Petronas Towers and their Islamic art-inspired design: In Kuala Lumpur, Malaysia, the Petronas Towers are designed with Islamic motifs, symbolizing the progress of the country.

The Colossus of Rhodes and its brief existence: One of the Seven Wonders of the Ancient World, the Colossus of Rhodes stood for only 56 years before being destroyed by an earthquake.

The Lotus Temple and its lotus flower shape: In Delhi, India, the Lotus Temple is designed in the shape of a lotus flower and serves as a place of worship for Bahá'ís.

La Casa Milà and its architectural controversy: Gaudí's Casa Milà in Barcelona was initially criticized for its avant-garde design, earning it the nickname "La Pedrera" (The Quarry).

The Fallingwater House and its functional design: Frank Lloyd Wright's Fallingwater House incorporates a natural waterfall flowing beneath the house.

The Duge Bridge and its dizzying height: The Duge Bridge in China is the world's highest suspension bridge, with towers rising over 565 meters above the Beipan River.

Unusual Atmospheric Phenomena

Investigate rare and extraordinary meteorological events.

Fish Rain: In certain places, like Yoro in Honduras, reports of fish rain exist, where fish fall from the sky during heavy storms.

Fata Morgana Mirage: A type of mirage that creates extraordinary optical illusions, such as floating cities or ships suspended in the air, due to light refraction.

Northern Lights (Polar Auroras): Luminous phenomena at the poles caused by solar particles colliding with the atmosphere. They can create colorful light displays in the sky.

Fire Tornado: This is a tornado that has absorbed flames from a wildfire, creating an extremely dangerous vortex of fire.

Ball Lightning: Electric discharges in the form of floating luminous balls that have been sighted during thunderstorms.

Lenticular Clouds: Saucer-shaped cloud formations that occur near mountains and are often mistaken for UFOs.

Circular Rainbow: A rare phenomenon in which a complete rainbow forms a circle around the observer, usually seen from an elevated position.

Red Rain or Snow: When rain or snow contains red dust particles, as occasionally happens in desert regions, it can be tinted red.

Devil's Winds: Extremely strong and short-duration wind gusts associated with severe thunderstorms.

Ice Circles: In cold climates, perfect circles of ice form on bodies of water, slowly rotating due to currents.

Marine Animal Rain: Similar to fish rain, some reports have documented the fall of octopuses and other marine animals during extreme weather events.

Mpemba Effect: A phenomenon in which hot water can freeze faster than cold water under certain conditions, though it remains a subject of scientific debate.

Blue Holes: Underwater sinkholes, known as blue holes, are deep-sea pits that appear to have an intense blue color due to the lack of light.

Catatumbo Lightning: Over Lake Maracaibo in Venezuela, a constant lightning known as the Catatumbo Lightning occurs, lasting up to 10 hours each night.

Fireballs: Meteoroids that are large and bright enough to be seen as fireballs in the sky during their entry into the atmosphere.

Arcus Roll Clouds: Roll-shaped clouds that stretch along the horizon and can be indicative of an imminent storm.

Dust Devils: Swirling columns of dust that form in arid areas, similar to tornadoes but without the presence of storm clouds.

22-Degree Halo: A solar halo that forms a circle around the sun when there are ice particles in the atmosphere refracting light.

Dry Fog: A phenomenon where fog appears to evaporate before reaching the ground, creating an illusion of moving fog.

Moon Illusion: An optical effect that makes the moon appear larger when near the horizon, despite its actual size not changing.

MYTHICAL CREATURES

Explore myths and legends about mythological beings from different cultures.

Cerberus – Guardian of the Underworld: In Greek mythology, Cerberus is a fierce three-headed dog that guards the entrance to the underworld, preventing the souls from leaving.

Kraken – Norse Sea Monster: Norse mythology features the Kraken, a colossal squid that, according to legends, lurks in the waters of northern Europe.

Chimera – Greek Hybrid Creature: The Chimera is a Greek mythological creature with a lion's head, a goat's body, and a snake's tail, representing the combination of different animals.

Unicorn – Symbol of Purity: Across various cultures, the unicorn is a mythical creature with a horn on its forehead and is often associated with purity and beauty.

Phoenix – Bird of Rebirth: In Egyptian and Greek mythology, the Phoenix is a bird that consumes itself in fire and then rises from its ashes, symbolizing immortality.

Sirens – Seductive Singers: Present in mythologies from various cultures, sirens are aquatic creatures with human appearance and mesmerizing songs, often associated with seduction and marine dangers.

Minotaur – Human Body, Bull's Head: In the labyrinth of King Minos in Greek mythology, the Minotaur, a creature with a human body and a bull's head, dwelled.

Dragons – From Asia to Europe: Dragons appear in mythologies worldwide, from the Eastern dragons of Chinese mythology to Western dragons, often depicted as winged serpents with fiery breath.

Werewolf – Lunar Curse: In various cultures, the werewolf is a human who transforms into a wolf, often associated with the full moon and the curse of lycanthropy.

Sphinx – Egyptian Enigma: The Sphinx of Giza, with a human head and a lion's body, is an architectural enigma that has puzzled researchers for centuries.

Kappa - Japanese Water Creature: In Japanese mythology, the Kappa is an aquatic creature with a dimple on its head that fills with water, granting it special powers.

Elves - Forest Guardians: Present in Norse and Celtic mythologies, elves are magical beings often associated with nature and the protection of forests.

Jinn - Beings from Arabian Mythology: Jinn are mythical creatures in Arabian mythology that possess magical abilities and can be either benevolent or malevolent.

Yeti - Abominable Snowman: In the legends of Tibet and the Himalayas, the Yeti is a creature similar to Bigfoot, associated with mountains and icy territories.

Centaur - Human-Horse of Greek Mythology: Centaurs have the upper body of a human and the lower body of a horse, often portrayed as wild and untamed beings.

Nagas – Sacred Snakes of Asia: In Hindu and Buddhist mythologies, Nagas are sacred snakes possessing both benevolent and malevolent aspects.

Chupacabra – Latin American Legend: In Latin American legends, the Chupacabra is a creature that feeds on the blood of livestock, often described as a reptilian being.

Birdman of Hopi Mythology: In the mythology of the Native American Hopi, the Birdman is a divine being associated with fertility and the agricultural cycle.

Banshee – Harbinger of Death: In Irish mythology, the Banshee is a female spirit that heralds death with her wail, often linked to specific lineages.

Chimera – Multiform Mythological Monster: In addition to the Greek Chimera, various cultures have created their own versions of the Chimera, a mythological being with parts of different animals.

117

Curiosities of the Underwater World

Get to know fascinating marine creatures and mysteries of the ocean depths

118

Migratory Freshwater Eel: The European eel, at the end of its life, undertakes an epic migration from Europe to the Sargasso Sea, where it spawns and dies.

The Immortal Jellyfish: Turritopsis dohrnii, a small jellyfish, is known as "the immortal" because it has the unique ability to reverse its aging process and rejuvenate.

Dumbo Octopus: This octopus is named for its ear-like fins resembling Dumbo's. It inhabits the depths and uses ear-shaped fins for swimming.

Under Extreme Pressure: In the depths of the ocean, the pressure is so intense that an unprotected human would be instantly crushed.

The Loudest Whale: The humpback whale is known for producing the loudest sounds in the animal kingdom, some of which can be heard thousands of kilometers away.

Mantis Shrimp and its Hunting Speed: The mantis shrimp has claws so powerful that they can move so fast they generate vapor bubbles, creating a devastating impact on their prey.

Ocean Fireflies: Some species of marine plankton, such as Noctiluca scintillans, can emit bioluminescent light, creating a light show in oceanic nights.

Sea Butterfly: The Clione limacina, nicknamed the "sea butterfly," is a species of sea slug that swims using wing-like flaps resembling butterfly wings.

Lanternfish: Some deep-sea fish have luminous organs called photophores that allow them to produce their own light in the dark depths.

The Great Barrier Reef: The Great Barrier Reef in Australia is the world's largest living structure, visible from space, and harbors an incredible diversity of marine life.

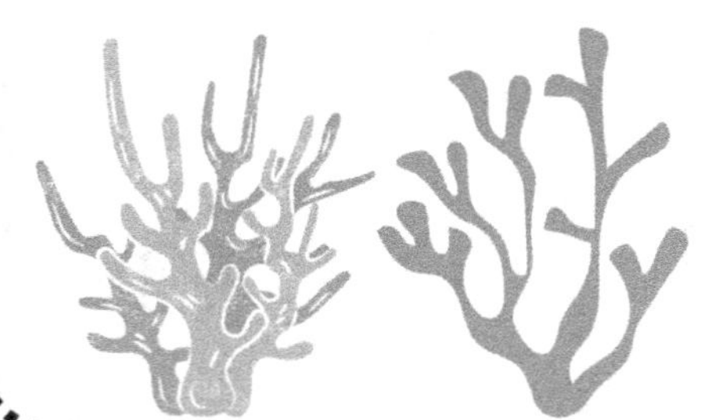
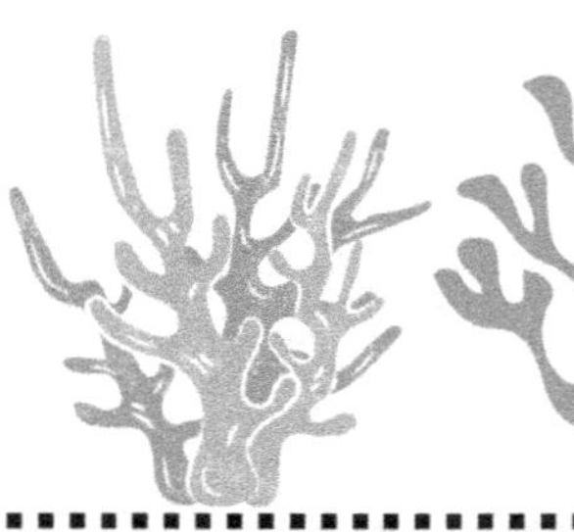

Jellyfish Light Show: The Atolla wyvillei jellyfish is capable of emitting flashes of light to attract predators and distract them while it escapes.

Anglerfish and its Hunting Method: The anglerfish, a camouflage master, uses an appendage on its head that mimics a lure to attract its prey before catching them.

Plastic Sea: In some oceanic areas, such as the North Pacific, a "soup" of decomposed plastic particles has formed, threatening marine life.

Titanic Wreck: At a depth of over 3,800 meters in the North Atlantic, the famous Titanic wreck was discovered in 1985.

Great Barrier Reef: Located off the northeast coast of Australia, it is the largest coral structure in the world and visible from space. This reef system, stretching for approximately 2,300 kilometers, harbors an incredible diversity of marine life, including thousands of fish species, corals, and other organisms. It is a unique and fragile ecosystem facing challenges due to climate change and human activity.

The Sex-changing Oyster: Some oyster species can change their gender based on the reproductive needs in their environment.

Whale Songs: Humpback whales produce complex songs that can last up to 30 minutes, believed to be part of courtship and communication.

Hydrothermal Vents: In the ocean depths, there are underwater thermal springs called hydrothermal vents that sustain unique ecosystems.

Transparent Abyssal Fish: The Macropinna microstoma is an abyssal fish with a transparent head and dome-shaped eyes, adapted for seeing in the darkness.

The Great Pacific Garbage Patch: In the Pacific Ocean, an extensive area of plastic waste known as the Great Pacific Garbage Patch has formed, impacting marine life and the ecosystem.

AMAZING WORLD RECORDS
EXPLORE FEATS AND ACHIEVEMENTS THAT HAVE SET WORLD RECORDS
123

The Fastest Man in the World: Usain Bolt, Jamaican athlete, set the world record for the 100 meters sprint with a time of 9.58 seconds in 2009.

Space Endurance Record: Russian cosmonaut Valeri Polyakov held the record for the longest stay in space, living aboard the Mir space station for 437 days and 18 hours.

Tallest Roller Coaster: The Kingda Ka at Six Flags Great Adventure in New Jersey, USA, holds the world record as the tallest roller coaster, standing at a height of 139 meters.

The Fastest Woman in the World: Florence Griffith-Joyner, known as Flo-Jo, has held the world records in the women's 100 meters and 200 meters since 1988.

Highest Parachute Jump: In 2012, Felix Baumgartner broke the record by jumping from an altitude of 39,045 meters, performing a freefall parachute jump.

The Fastest Swimmer: American swimmer Michael Phelps holds the record for the most Olympic medals, with 23 gold, 3 silver, and 2 bronze.

Longest Non-Stop Flight Record: In 2020, Qantas QF7879 set a new record by flying non-stop from New York to Sydney, covering 16,200 kilometers in approximately 19 hours and 16 minutes.

Tallest Recorded Man: Robert Wadlow, known as "the Alton giant," reached a height of 2.72 meters before his death at the age of 22.

Longest Javelin Throw Record: Czech athlete Jan Železný holds the world record for javelin throw with a distance of 98.48 meters, set in 1996.

World's Largest Bicycle: The largest recorded bicycle measures 20.07 meters in length and was created in the city of Haren, Germany.

The Longest Pizza: In Naples, Italy, a pizza measuring 1,853.88 meters in length was made in 2016, setting a world record.

Highest Parachute Jump from the Stratosphere: Alan Eustace, Google's vice president, performed a parachute jump from the stratosphere in 2014, establishing the record for the longest free fall from 41.4 kilometers high.

Fastest Ascent of Mount Everest: Italian climber Reinhold Messner and Austrian Peter Habeler made the fastest ascent of Mount Everest without supplemental oxygen in 1978.

World's Largest Cake: In 2011, in the city of Chengdu, China, a giant cake weighing over 8,800 kilograms was created.

Longest Hammer Throw Record: The world record for men's hammer throw is 86.74 meters, set by Russian athlete Yuriy Sedykh in 1986.

Fastest Bicycle Trip Around the World: In 2017, Mark Beaumont completed his journey around the world on a bicycle in 79 days, 44 minutes.

Most Push-Ups in 24 Hours: Charles Servizio set the world record by performing 46,001 push-ups in 24 hours in 1993.

Longest Escalator: In Hong Kong, the Central-Mid-Levels Escalator is the world's longest, spanning a distance of 800 meters.

Deepest Pool: The Y-40 Deep Joy pool in Italy is the world's deepest pool, reaching a depth of 42 meters.

Most Dominoes Toppled: In 2009, a team of domino builders set the world record by toppling 4,491,863 dominoes during an event in the Netherlands.

SURVIVOR STORIES

DISCOVER NARRATIVES OF SURVIVAL IN EXTREME SITUATIONS AND ADVERSITY

Pacific Island Castaway: In 1942, Japanese soldier Hiroo Onoda was discovered on a Philippine island, unaware that World War II had ended. He spent 29 years hiding and fighting as a guerrilla.

The Andes Odyssey: In 1972, a group of Uruguayan rugby players survived 72 days in the Andes after their plane crashed. They resorted to cannibalism to save some of their fellow survivors.

Man Trapped by a Boulder: In 2003, Aron Ralston became trapped in a Utah canyon and, after five days, had to amputate part of his arm to free himself.

Deadly Winter in the Sierra Nevada: In 1846, the Donner Party got stranded in the Sierra Nevada due to heavy snowfall. They resorted to cannibalism to survive during the winter.

Shark Attack: In 1916, a shark attack in New Jersey inspired Peter Benchley's novel "Jaws" and Steven Spielberg's movie.

Surviving a Bear Attack: In 2003, mountaineer Aaron Ralston (previously mentioned) survived a bear attack in Colorado before his famous canyon incident.

Uganda Hostage Crisis: In 1976, a group of Israelis was kidnapped and held hostage in Entebbe, Uganda. A successful rescue operation was carried out.

Trapped in a Cave in Thailand: In 2018, a youth soccer team became trapped in a flooded cave in Thailand. All were successfully rescued after a complex international rescue operation.

Andes Plane Crash: In 1972, Uruguayan Air Force Flight 571 crashed in the Andes. The survivors had to resort to cannibalism to survive.

Escape from a Concentration Camp: British prisoner of war Airey Neave managed to escape from a Nazi concentration camp during World War II and reach freedom.

Desert Survival: In 2003, American hiker Aron Ralston became trapped in a canyon in Utah and had to amputate part of his arm to survive.

Uruguayan Air Force Flight 571: In 1972, survivors of the Uruguayan Air Force Flight 571 crash had to resort to cannibalism to survive while awaiting rescue.

Tasman Sea Rescue: In 1998, British yachtsman Tony Bullimore was rescued in the Tasman Sea after spending four days trapped in his overturned boat.

Man Who Survived Two Atomic Bombs: Tsutomu Yamaguchi, a Japanese citizen, survived both the Hiroshima and Nagasaki atomic bombings during World War II.

China Landslide: In 2008, a Chinese man was trapped underground for 36 hours after a landslide. He was successfully rescued.

Pacific Ocean Pilot: Louis Zamperini, a World War II pilot, survived 47 days on a life raft in the Pacific Ocean before being captured by the Japanese.

Indian Ocean Castaway: In 2012, fisherman José Salvador Alvarenga survived 438 days adrift in the Indian Ocean after his boat drifted off course.

Antarctic Shipwreck: Ernest Shackleton led an expedition in 1914 that became trapped in the ice of Antarctica. Despite the adversities, all members of the expedition survived.

Surviving the Tsunami in Thailand: In 2004, Czech model Petra Nemcova survived the tsunami in Thailand by clinging to a tree for hours before being rescued.

Desert Endurance Race: Italian runner Mauro Prosperi got lost during a race in the Sahara Desert in 1994 and survived by drinking his own urine before being rescued.

Celebration Traditions around the World

Learn about unique festivities and celebrations from various cultures

Holi in India: Holi is a Hindu festival known as the "Festival of Colors," where people throw colored powder and celebrate the arrival of spring.

San Fermín Festival in Spain: The San Fermín festival in Pamplona is famous for the running of the bulls, where participants run ahead of bulls through the streets.

Lantern Festival in Taiwan: The Lantern Festival, marking the end of the Chinese New Year, is celebrated with lantern parades and displays of ornamental lanterns.

Diwali in India: Diwali, also known as the Festival of Lights, is a Hindu celebration involving lights, fireworks, and the lighting of clay lamps.

Oktoberfest in Germany: Oktoberfest is the world's largest beer festival, celebrated in Munich, Germany, with music, food, and, of course, beer.

Day of the Dead in Mexico: The Day of the Dead is a Mexican holiday where the deceased are honored with offerings, food, and colorful celebrations in cemeteries.

Lantern Festival in Thailand: The Lantern Festival, known as Loy Krathong, is celebrated in Thailand with the release of paper lanterns into rivers to ward off bad luck.

Chinese New Year: Chinese New Year celebrations include parades, fireworks, and cultural activities to welcome the new lunar year.

Rio de Janeiro Carnival in Brazil: The Rio Carnival is one of the largest and most colorful in the world, featuring parades, music, and street dances.

Cherry Blossom Festival in Japan: Hanami is the Japanese tradition of appreciating the beauty of cherry blossoms during the blooming season.

Christmas in Iceland: In Iceland, Christmas is celebrated with thirteen "Yule Lads," mischievous versions of Santa Claus, who visit homes leaving gifts or potatoes based on children's behavior.

Songkran Water Festival in Thailand: Songkran marks the Thai New Year with water festivals, where people splash water on each other in the streets.

La Tomatina in Spain: In Buñol, Spain, La Tomatina is a festival where participants throw tomatoes at each other in a massive food fight.

Burning Man in the United States: Burning Man is a countercultural event in the Nevada desert, where a temporary city is built, and a giant sculpture is burned at the end of the festival.

Beaujolais Wine Festival in France: The third Thursday of November marks the release of Beaujolais Nouveau, celebrated with festivities and wine tastings throughout France.

Full Moon Festival in Thailand: During the full moon of November, the Loy Krathong and Yi Peng Lantern Festival light up the skies of Thailand with floating lanterns and flying lanterns.

Dragon Boat Festival in China: This festival is celebrated with dragon boat races to commemorate the death of the Chinese poet Qu Yuan.

Spring Festival in Uzbekistan: Navruz, the arrival of spring, is celebrated with festivals, parades, and cultural events in Uzbekistan.

Lantern Festival in China: Yuanxiao Jie marks the end of the Lantern Festival with the release of flying lanterns into the Chinese sky to ward off evil spirits.

St. John's Day in Spain: Celebrated on the eve of the summer solstice, St. John's night is celebrated with bonfires, music, and dances on Spanish beaches.

137

Curiosities of Extreme Sports

Extreme activities that defy physical and mental limits

138

Wingsuit Flying: Wingsuit flying practitioners wear special suits that allow them to glide through the air, defying gravity as they descend at high speeds.

Base Jumping: Base jumping involves leaping from fixed structures, such as cliffs or bridges, with a parachute for a free fall before deploying the parachute.

Free Solo Climbing: Free solo climbers ascend rock walls without ropes or protection, relying solely on their skill and courage.

Parachute Jump without a Parachute: In 2016, skydiver Luke Aikins made a parachute jump from 7,620 meters without wearing a parachute, landing safely in a specially designed net.

Bungee Jumping from a Helicopter: In Queenstown, New Zealand, bungee jumping from a helicopter is offered, taking the experience to a whole new level.

Free Solo Climbing: Free solo climbing involves ascending cliffs and vertical walls without ropes or safety equipment, relying solely on the climber's physical and mental skills.

Canyoneering: In canyoneering, adventurers navigate narrow gorges, jump waterfalls, and swim through watery obstacles in rugged terrains.

Extreme Mountain Biking: Extreme mountain bikers descend steep and hazardous terrains, overcoming natural obstacles and performing spectacular jumps.

Parkour: Parkour practitioners move through urban environments, overcoming obstacles with fluid, agile, and rapid movements, defying gravity.

Hang Gliding: Hang gliding pilots fly using non-motorized gliders, harnessing air currents to glide through the sky.

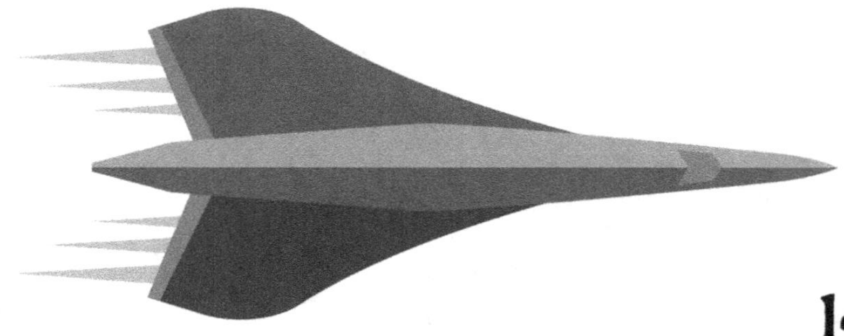

Extreme Skiing: Extreme skiing takes skiers to steep and perilous terrains, where they confront extreme weather conditions and challenging landscapes.

Big Wave Surfing: In big wave surfing, surfers tackle giant waves in locations like Nazaré, Portugal, challenging the force of the ocean.

Acrobatic Water Skiing: Acrobatic water skiing combines water skiing and acrobatics, with skiers performing tricks and jumps on the water.

Ice Climbing: Ice climbers tackle steep and icy routes, using tools such as crampons and ice axes to ascend.

Freestyle Motocross: In freestyle motocross, riders perform spectacular jumps and tricks on specially designed ramps, defying gravity.

White Water Rafting: Adventurers engage in white water rafting, navigating turbulent and challenging rapids in high-speed rivers.

Extreme Obstacle Course Racing: Extreme obstacle course races, such as the Spartan Race and Tough Mudder, challenge participants with rugged terrain and challenging obstacles.

Snowkiting: Snowkiting practitioners use kites to travel across snow, allowing them to perform jumps and spectacular maneuvers.

Torchlit Base Jumping: Some base jumpers execute jumps with lit torches in hand, creating striking visuals during the descent.

Paraskiing: In paraskiing, skiers are towed by parachutes as they descend snowy slopes, combining skiing with the thrill of flight.

CURIOSITIES ABOUT FAMOUS ATHLETES

Michael Jordan and Baseball: After retiring from basketball in 1993, Michael Jordan surprised the world by attempting a professional baseball career, playing for the Birmingham Barons, a minor league team affiliated with the Chicago White Sox.

Usain Bolt and his McNuggets love: Jamaican sprinter Usain Bolt is known for his incredible speed, but also for his love of McDonald's chicken McNuggets before competitions.

Nadal and his bottle ritual: Spanish tennis player Rafael Nadal has a ritual before each match: he meticulously aligns his water bottles along the baseline of the court.

Michael Phelps and his astonishing diet: Swimmer Michael Phelps, during his training for the Olympic Games, consumed around 12,000 calories a day, including a significant amount of pasta and pizzas.

Serena Williams and Swimwear Fear: Despite being a tennis champion, Serena Williams had a fear of swimwear in her childhood and brought her mother to competitions to distract her from the pressure.

Lionel Messi and Growth Hormone: Lionel Messi was treated with growth hormone as a child due to his short stature, a medical condition known as growth hormone deficiency.

Tom Brady and Strategic Diet: NFL quarterback Tom Brady follows a highly restrictive diet that excludes foods like tomatoes, peppers, eggplants, and mushrooms due to their lectin content.

Simone Biles and Gymnastics Records: Simone Biles is the most decorated gymnast in the history of the World Championships, with a total of 25 medals, 19 of them gold.

Roger Federer and Banana Aversion: Despite being a common source of energy for athletes, Roger Federer does not eat bananas and avoids them before and during matches.

Cristiano Ronaldo and Devotion to Training: Cristiano Ronaldo is known for his exceptional work ethic and dedication to training, often practicing beyond scheduled hours with his team.

Danica Patrick and Love for Speed: Danica Patrick, a racing driver, is the only woman in history to win an IndyCar series race and the first to lead the Indianapolis 500.

Muhammad Ali and Civil Rights Advocacy: Ali was a prominent advocate for civil rights and refused to be drafted into the military during the Vietnam War, leading to the suspension of his boxing world title and a criminal conviction.

Ronda Rousey and Judo Dominance: Ronda Rousey won a gold medal in judo at the 2004 Athens Olympics before becoming a trailblazer in mixed martial arts (MMA).

LeBron James and Generosity: LeBron James is known for his philanthropic efforts and established the LeBron James Family Foundation, which has funded college scholarships and community projects.

Mia Hamm and Impact on Women's Soccer: Mia Hamm, former American soccer player, is one of the most influential figures in the history of women's soccer and has been a consistent advocate for the sport's development.

Kobe Bryant and Achievements in the NBA: Kobe Bryant, basketball legend, won five NBA championships with the Los Angeles Lakers and retired with two retired numbers, 8 and 24.

Venus and Serena Williams and Tennis Dominance: The Williams sisters, Venus and Serena, have been dominant in women's tennis, winning numerous individual and doubles titles throughout their careers.

Tiger Woods and Impact on Golf: Tiger Woods is one of the most successful and well-known golfers in history, having won numerous major titles and revolutionized the sport.

Muhammad Ali and Birth Name: Muhammad Ali was born as Cassius Marcellus Clay Jr. and changed his name after converting to Islam in 1975.

Nadia Comăneci and Olympic Perfection: This Romanian gymnast made history at the 1976 Olympic Games by receiving the first perfect score of 10.0 in the history of artistic gymnastics. During the Montreal Olympic Games in Canada on July 18, 1976, Nadia Comăneci achieved this milestone in her uneven bars routine. Comăneci's astonishing performance left the judges astounded, as her execution was deemed flawless with no apparent errors.

Nadia Comăneci's feat not only marked a historic moment in gymnastics but also changed the perception of what was considered possible in the sport. Her success highlighted the pursuit of perfection in athletic performance and became a role model for subsequent generations of gymnasts. Nadia Comăneci won a total of three gold medals at the 1976 Games, becoming an Olympic icon and an inspiration for athletes worldwide.

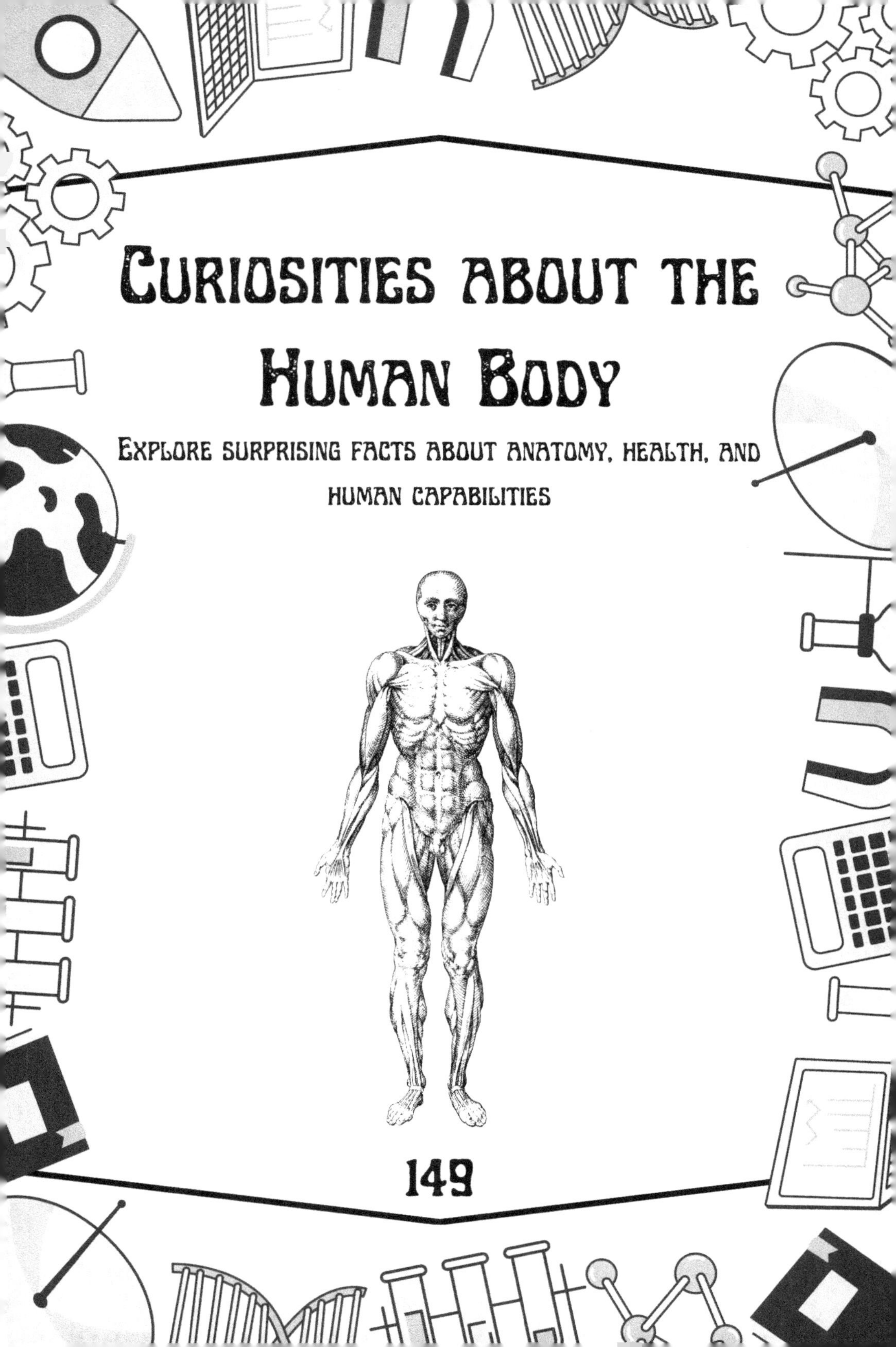

Curiosities about the Human Body

Explore surprising facts about anatomy, health, and human capabilities

149

Ever-Changing Skeletal System: The human skeleton undergoes complete renewal approximately every 10 years due to the bone renewal process.

Saliva Generation: Throughout life, a person can produce enough saliva to fill two Olympic-sized swimming pools.

Resilient Hair: Human hair is surprisingly strong. A single hair strand can withstand the weight of a small apple.

Constant Skin Renewal: Over a lifetime, a person loses about 18 kilograms of skin as dead skin cells shed and are constantly replaced.

Unique Tongue: Each person has a unique tongue print, similar to fingerprints, making each tongue distinct in terms of grooves and patterns.

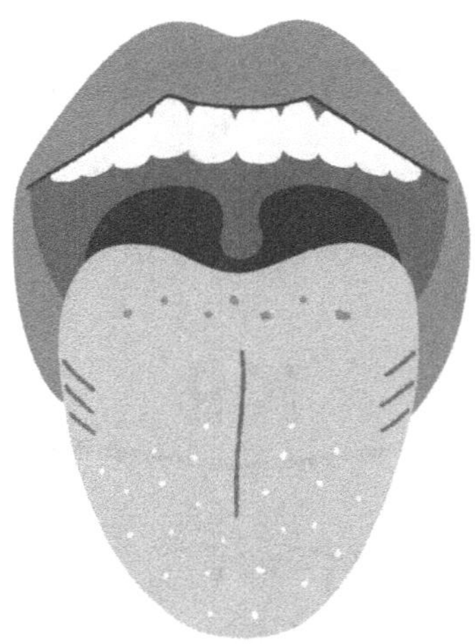

Total Length of Blood Vessels: If all the blood vessels in the human body were laid end to end, they would reach a length of approximately 100,000 kilometers.

Thumb Dexterity: The ability of the thumb to touch each finger on the hand is a unique feature of humans and is key to our manual skills.

Visual Response Time: The average time it takes the human eye to process an image and send a signal to the brain is as short as 13 milliseconds.

Brain Weight: Despite representing only 2% of the total body weight, the human brain uses about 20% of the body's energy and oxygen.

REM Sleep Cycle: Over an average lifetime, a person spends around 25 years sleeping, and approximately 6 of those years are in the REM (rapid eye movement) sleep phase.

Unique Smell Print: Each person has a unique body odor, except for identical twins, who share the same smell print.

Bones in the Middle Ear: The stapes, the smallest bone in the human body, is located in the middle ear and measures approximately 0.1 centimeters.

Individual Nose: Each nose has a unique dimple pattern, similar to fingerprints.

Sneezing Speed: The average speed of a sneeze is around 160 kilometers per hour, and the force of a sneeze can propel germs up to a distance of 7 meters.

Length of the Small Intestine: Despite its narrowness, the small intestine has an average length of 6 meters, facilitating the absorption of nutrients.

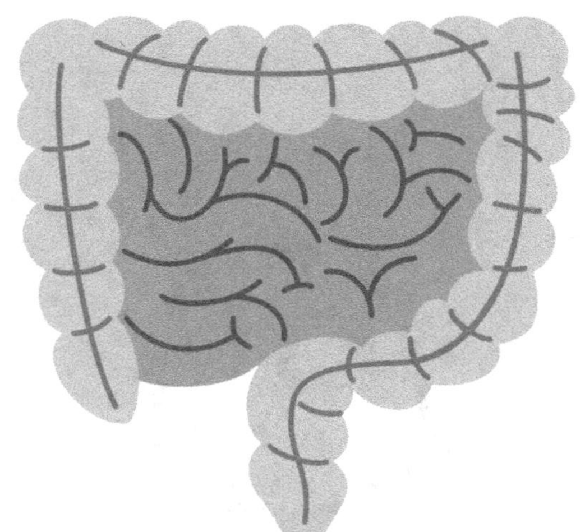

Liver Regeneration: The liver is the only organ in the human body capable of fully regenerating. It can grow back even after losing up to 75% of its mass.

Pressure Points in the Body: There are at least 6 points on the human body where, if enough pressure were applied, a person could temporarily faint due to the lack of blood flow to the brain.

Daily Blinking Rate: On average, a person blinks about 15 times per minute, adding up to a total of approximately 14,000 blinks daily.

Length of Nails: If all the nails of a person were cut and placed side by side, they would reach a length of several meters.

Stomach Acid: The gastric acid in the stomach is strong enough to dissolve metals like zinc. However, the mucous layer of the stomach prevents this acid from damaging the stomach walls.

EXTRAORDINARY LOVE STORIES
DISCOVER NOTABLE AND TOUCHING ROMANCES THROUGHOUT HISTORY.
154

Romeo and Juliet: The tragic love story between Romeo and Juliet, written by William Shakespeare in the 16th century, remains one of the most well-known and performed love stories in literature and theater.

Tristan and Isolde: A medieval legend that tells the tale of forbidden love between Tristan, a knight of King Arthur's Round Table, and Isolde, the wife of his uncle.

Cleopatra and Mark Antony: Cleopatra, the last queen of Egypt, and Mark Antony, a Roman general, shared a passionate romance that had significant political consequences.

Pierre and Marie Curie: The love story and scientific collaboration between Pierre and Marie Curie led to the discovery of radium and polonium, earning them both the Nobel Prize in Physics in 1903.

John and Abigail Adams: The correspondence between the second President of the United States, John Adams, and his wife Abigail is known for being passionate and revealing, showcasing their strong bond despite adversities.

Frida Kahlo and Diego Rivera: Mexican artists Frida Kahlo and Diego Rivera had a tumultuous marriage, but their love and passion for art kept them connected throughout the years.

Eloise and Abelard: The medieval tale of Abelard and Eloise is a tragic romance between a philosopher and his student, marked by Abelard's castration and Eloise's subsequent monastic life.

Edward VIII and Wallis Simpson: King Edward VIII abdicated the British throne in 1936 to marry Wallis Simpson, an American divorcee, defying social norms and royal tradition.

Carl and Ellie Fredricksen (Up): Although fictional, the characters from the Disney-Pixar movie "Up," Carl and Ellie, touched audiences of all ages with their beautiful love story and loss.

Abelard and Heloise (Film): The movie "Eternal Sunshine of the Spotless Mind" tells the story of Joel and Clementine, who try to erase memories of their failed relationship.

Jane Austen and Tom Lefroy: The famous author Jane Austen had a brief but passionate romance with Tom Lefroy, an Irish law student, which influenced her literary work.

Paul Newman and Joanne Woodward: The acting duo Paul Newman and Joanne Woodward enjoyed a long-lasting and successful Hollywood marriage that lasted for over 50 years until Newman's death.

Jackie and John F. Kennedy: The marriage of Jackie and John F. Kennedy was closely followed by the public and marked by moments of romance and tragedy, such as JFK's assassination in 1963.

Lancelot and Guinevere: The Arthurian legend includes the tale of the forbidden love between Sir Lancelot and Queen Guinevere, the wife of King Arthur.
Bonnie and Clyde: Bonnie Parker and Clyde Barrow were criminal lovers who lived a life of crime during the Great Depression, eventually being shot dead by the police in 1934.

Prince Rainier III and Grace Kelly: Prince Rainier III of Monaco and actress Grace Kelly had a fairytale wedding in 1956, uniting royalty and Hollywood glamour.

Elizabeth Barrett and Robert Browning: The epistolary relationship between poets Elizabeth Barrett and Robert Browning blossomed into a deep and enduring love, despite opposition from Elizabeth's family.

Guinevere and Lancelot: Another tale from Arthurian legend, the romance between Queen Guinevere and Sir Lancelot led to the downfall of the Round Table and the death of Arthur.

Prince and Apollonia Kotero (Purple Rain): The movie "Purple Rain" tells the love story between Prince and Apollonia Kotero, becoming a cultural icon in the 1980s.

Marc Antony and Cleopatra (Movie): The cinematic portrayal of the relationship between Marc Antony and Cleopatra, as seen in the 1963 film "Cleopatra" starring Elizabeth Taylor and Richard Burton.

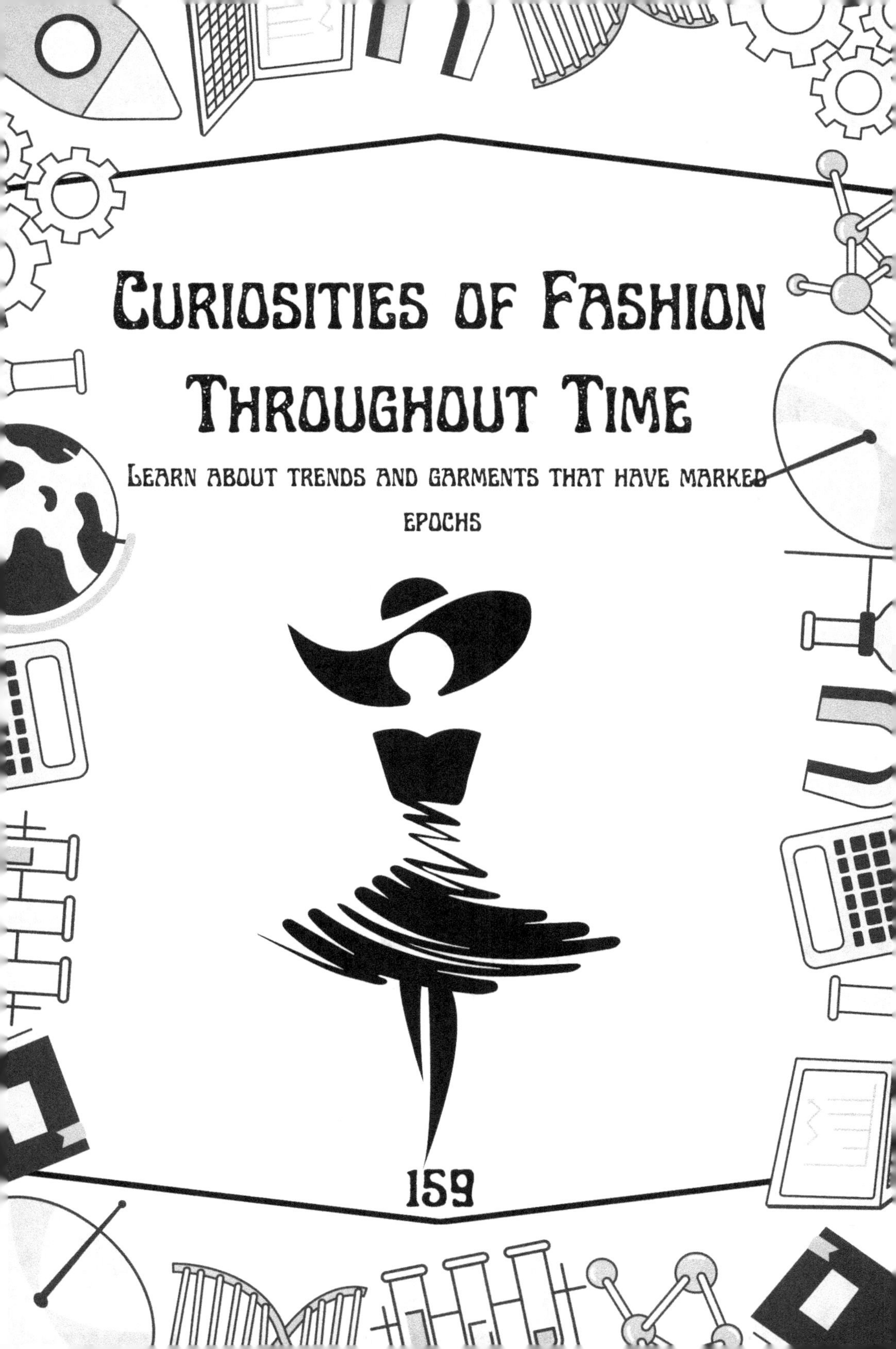

Curiosities of Fashion Throughout Time

Learn about trends and garments that have marked epochs

Wigs in Ancient Rome: In Ancient Rome, women wore elaborate wigs made from human hair, animal hair, or even wool as a symbol of social status and beauty.

Renaissance Fashion: During the Renaissance, women sought to have a pale complexion, often using arsenic powder on their faces, which sometimes resulted in health issues due to the toxicity of arsenic.

Leggings in the 16th Century: In the 16th century, leggings—tight-fitting pieces of fabric that covered the legs and feet—were popular for both men and women as a way to display status and fashion.

Corsets in the Victorian Era: In the Victorian era, corsets were popular and tightened to extreme limits to achieve a tiny waist, often at the expense of women's health.

Platform Shoes in the 1970s: 1970s fashion brought about platform shoes, which reached extraordinary heights and were popular among both men and women.

Jeans and the Youth Revolution: Jeans became popular in the 1950s as a symbol of youth rebellion, especially associated with rock and roll culture and counterculture.

Paco Rabanne's Space Age Suits: In the 1960s, designer Paco Rabanne created futuristic space suits using metallic and plastic materials, influencing futuristic fashion during that period.

Bell-Bottom Pants of the 60s and 70s: The trend of bell-bottom pants in the 1960s and 1970s was an expression of counterculture and the liberation from traditional fashion constraints.

Mary Quant's Mini Skirt: British designer Mary Quant popularized the mini skirt in the 1960s, marking a milestone in fashion and reflecting women's liberation.

Punk Fashion in the 70s and 80s: Punk fashion, characterized by torn clothing, imperfections, and bold accessories, emerged as an expression of rebellion and anti-establishment in the 70s and 80s.

Logomania Design in the 90s: In the 1990s, logomania was at its peak, with prominent brands showcasing their logos prominently on clothing and accessories.

Jackie Kennedy's "Pillbox" Hats: Jackie Kennedy popularized the elegant "Pillbox" hats during the 1960s, turning them into a fashion icon of the era.

"Flapper" Dresses in the 20s: 1920s fashion included short and loose "flapper" dresses, challenging conventions of previous fashion and reflecting women's liberation.

Tracksuits and Sportswear: In the 1980s, tracksuits and sportswear became popular beyond the sports realm, becoming a casual fashion trend.

Backwards Baseball Caps: In the 1990s, the trend of wearing baseball caps backward became popular thanks to figures in hip-hop and youth culture.

Camouflage Clothing: Camouflage fashion, inspired by military clothing, became a trend in urban fashion from the 1990s onward.

Hippie and the 60s Counterculture: 1960s hippie fashion was characterized by loose garments, vibrant colors, natural fabrics, and psychedelic elements, reflecting the spirit of the counterculture.

Platform Shoes in the 90s: Platform shoe fashion experienced a resurgence in the 1990s, with thick and eye-catching soles associated with grunge culture and alternative style.

Steampunk Fashion: Steampunk fashion, inspired by Victorian aesthetics and the era of the Industrial Revolution, uniquely combines antique and futuristic elements.

Japanese Designer Clothing: Japanese designers such as Issey Miyake and Rei Kawakubo have influenced global fashion with their innovative and conceptual designs since the 1980s.

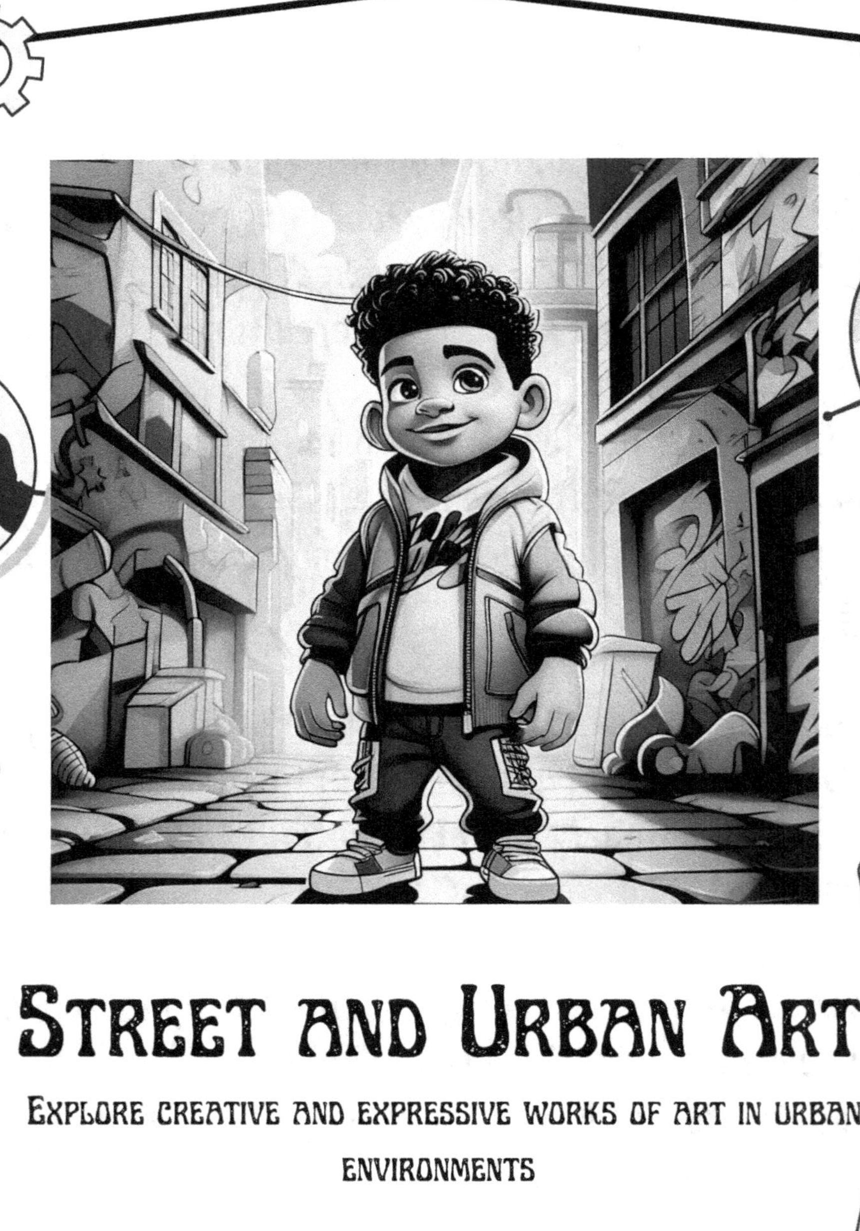

Street and Urban Art

Explore creative and expressive works of art in urban environments

Origins of Graffiti: Modern graffiti has its roots in the 1960s in Philadelphia and New York, where young people began to sign their names and nicknames on city walls.

Banksy and His Mystery: Banksy, a famous street artist, keeps his identity a secret. Although various theories have been speculated, his anonymity contributes to his mysterious aura.

3D Street Art: Artists like Julian Beever and Edgar Mueller create 3D illusions on the streets, using shading and perspective techniques to deceive the eye and give the illusion of depth.

Stencils and Templates: Many street artists use stencils or templates to create detailed and replicable works quickly in urban environments.

Urban Art Festival in Bristol: Upfest in Bristol, UK, is one of the largest street art festivals in the world, attracting street artists from around the globe.

165

Graffiti and Hip-Hop: Graffiti and hip-hop are closely linked in their origins; both emerged in the 1970s in New York and share a cultural and artistic connection.

Social Muralism: Urban art often addresses social and political issues. Murals like those by Diego Rivera in Mexico inspired a tradition of social muralism that continues today.

Urban Interventions: Urban artists often perform creative interventions in urban spaces, transforming everyday objects into works of art, such as stairs, traffic signs, and trash containers.

Abandoned Spaces: Many street art artists find inspiration in abandoned spaces, using walls and disused structures as canvases for their works.

Invader's Work: The artist Invader is known for his Space Invaders mosaics, which he has placed in cities worldwide. His identity is also unknown.

Art in Motion: Some urban artists use temporary art forms, such as water painting on dry streets, creating works that disappear over time.

JR's Work and Social Action: Artist JR combines urban art with social action, creating giant portraits of people and placing them in public spaces to highlight social and humanitarian issues.

Bicycles as Canvases: In some cities, abandoned bicycles become canvases for urban artists, transforming them into works of art rather than waste.

Art in Public Spaces: Street art aims to move away from traditional gallery and museum spaces, bringing artistic expression directly to public spaces that are accessible to everyone.

Ephemeral Sculptures: Some street art artists create ephemeral sculptures using temporary materials like snow, sand, or even fallen leaves.

POW! WOW! Festival: The POW! WOW! festival is an urban art and mural festival held in various cities around the world, bringing together artists to transform entire communities with their works.

Art on Crosswalks: Some cities incorporate art on crosswalks, turning them into colorful and creative pieces that transform the experience of crossing the street.

Street Art and Technology: Some street art artists use technology, such as augmented reality, to create interactive experiences that merge the digital and physical worlds.

Giant Mural Paintings: Cities like Wynwood in Miami feature giant murals covering entire buildings, turning them into authentic outdoor art galleries.

Shepard Fairey's Work: Shepard Fairey, the creator of the famous "Hope" poster of Barack Obama, is an influential urban artist who addresses social and political themes in his works.

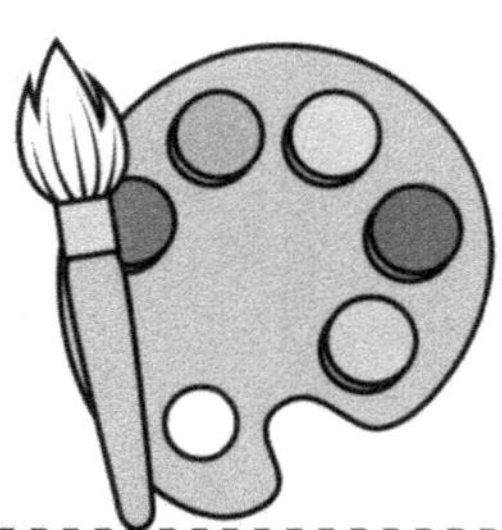

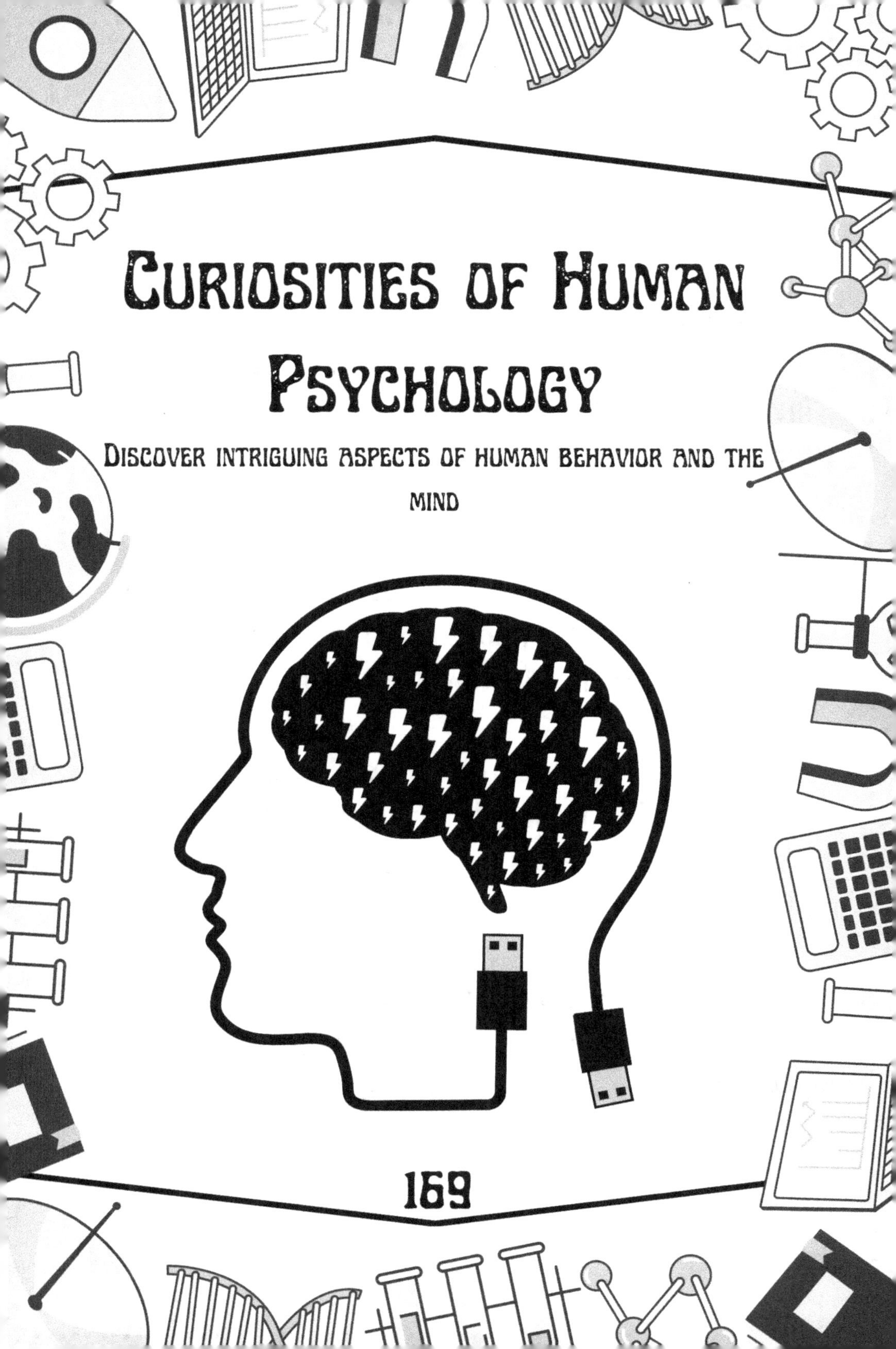

CURIOSITIES OF HUMAN PSYCHOLOGY
DISCOVER INTRIGUING ASPECTS OF HUMAN BEHAVIOR AND THE MIND
169

Placebo Effect: The positive response to an inert treatment, known as the placebo effect, highlights the power of the mind in health perception and symptom relief.

Social Cognition: Social cognition refers to how we process, store, and apply social information. It involves understanding emotions, empathy, and interpreting social signals.

Stockholm Syndrome: It is a psychological phenomenon in which victims develop an emotional connection with their captors, often defending them and showing sympathy towards them.

Primacy and Recency Effect: First and last impressions have a significant impact on judgment formation. This phenomenon is known as the primacy and recency effect.

Flashbulb Memory: Flashbulb memory refers to the ability to recall vivid details of significant events, such as the location and emotions experienced, despite the passage of time.

Efecto Dunning-Kruger: Individuals with limited abilities often overestimate their competence, while highly skilled individuals tend to underestimate their abilities. This phenomenon is known as the Dunning-Kruger effect.

Multitasking Effect: Contrary to common belief, multitasking can decrease productivity and the quality of work, as attention is divided among several tasks.

Cognitive Dissonance Theory: The cognitive dissonance theory posits that people feel discomfort when their beliefs and actions are in conflict, leading them to change their attitudes to alleviate the discomfort.

Halo Effect: This phenomenon occurs when a positive or negative impression of a particular characteristic of a person influences the overall evaluation of that person.

Pygmalion Effect: Also known as the self-fulfilling prophecy, the Pygmalion effect refers to how others' expectations can influence a person's performance.

Paradox of Choice: Although having options is positive, the paradox of choice suggests that too many choices can lead to anxiety and dissatisfaction instead of happiness.

Conformity Effect: The tendency to change our beliefs and behaviors to fit in with the majority is known as the conformity effect, highlighting social influence on our decisions.

Cabin Fever Syndrome: After a period of confinement or restriction, some individuals may develop cabin fever syndrome, experiencing anxiety when facing the outside world.

Illusion of Transparency: People tend to overestimate the visibility of their internal emotions, falsely believing that others can easily perceive their feelings.

Fat Band Effect: Background music can influence people's perception of wait time in a location, known as the fat band effect.

Tourette's Syndrome and Creativity: Some studies suggest that people with Tourette's syndrome may experience an increase in creativity due to the connection between the brain circuits involved in both.

False Consensus Phenomenon: People tend to overestimate the number of individuals who agree with them, erroneously assuming that their opinions are more widely shared than they actually are.

Nature Deficit Syndrome: The lack of connection with nature can have negative impacts on mental health and well-being, a phenomenon known as nature deficit syndrome.

Zeigarnik Effect: People tend to remember incomplete tasks more easily than completed ones, known as the Zeigarnik effect.

Mere Exposure Effect: The tendency to develop a preference for something simply because it has been encountered repeatedly is known as the mere exposure effect.

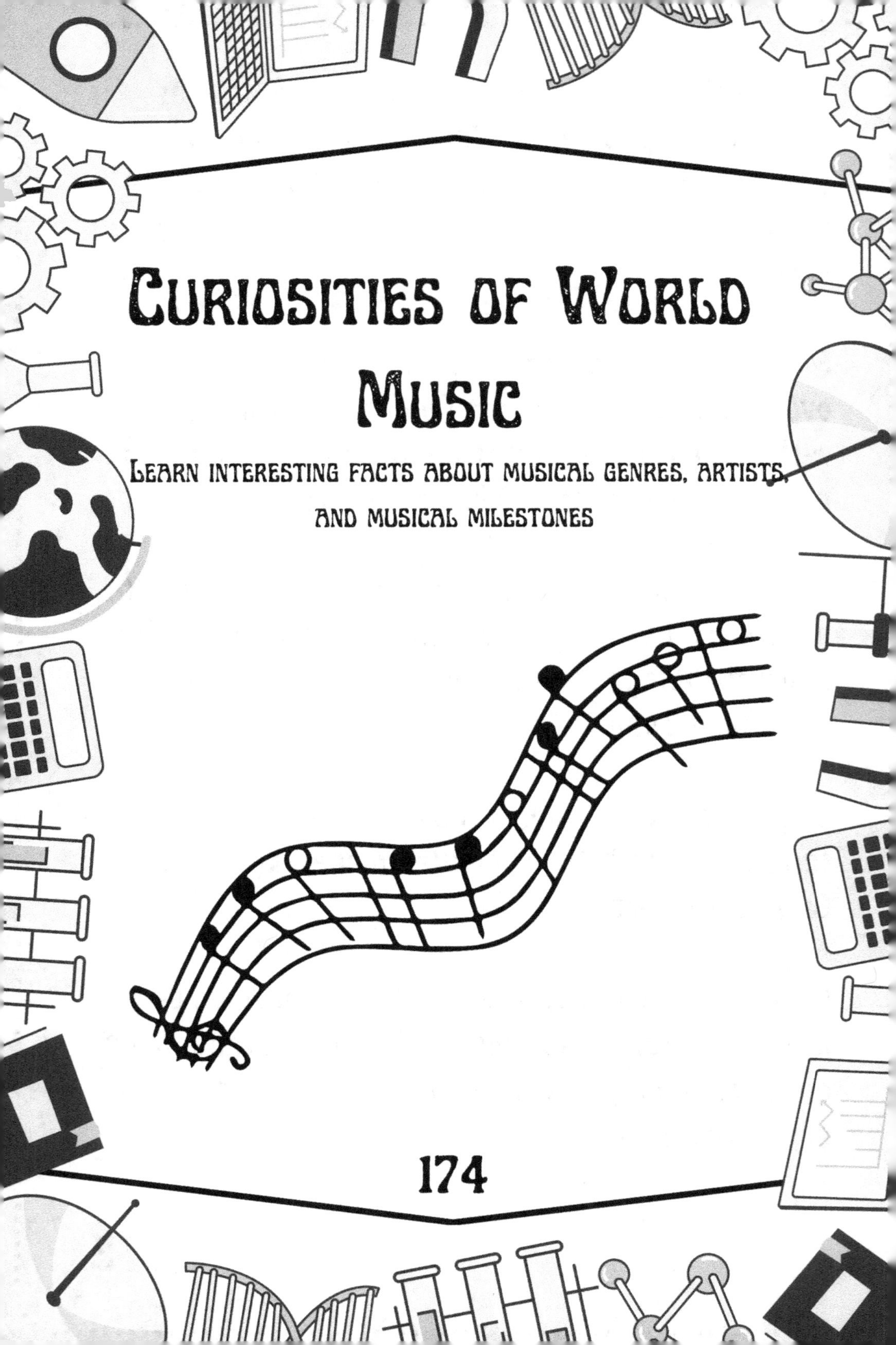

CURIOSITIES OF WORLD MUSIC
LEARN INTERESTING FACTS ABOUT MUSICAL GENRES, ARTISTS, AND MUSICAL MILESTONES
174

Origins of Jazz: Jazz, a distinctive musical genre of the United States, has its roots in the fusion of African and European musical traditions and developed in New Orleans in the late 19th century.

King of Rock and Roll: Elvis Presley, known as the "King of Rock and Roll," was a trailblazer in blending musical genres, merging blues, country, and rock in his music.

Freddie Mercury's Record: Freddie Mercury, the lead vocalist of Queen, is renowned for his four-octave vocal range, one of the widest in the history of music.

Musical Genre of Bob Marley: Bob Marley popularized reggae globally, blending elements of ska and rocksteady to create a distinctive sound that conveyed messages of peace and social justice.

Jimi Hendrix's Guitar: Jimi Hendrix, one of the greatest guitarists in history, played his guitar left-handed and reversed it to suit his unique style.

175

Mozart and Deafness: Despite composing some of his masterpieces while deaf, Mozart continued creating music until his final days.

Mariah Carey's Record: Mariah Carey holds the record for the single with the longest run at number one on the Billboard Hot 100 with "One Sweet Day," which spent 16 weeks at the top.

Bach and His Numerous Compositions: Johann Sebastian Bach, the Baroque composer, produced over a thousand compositions throughout his life, ranging from liturgical pieces to keyboard masterpieces.

The Realm of Indie Music: The term "indie" comes from "independent," and indie music refers to the independent production and distribution of music, moving away from major record labels.

K-Pop Genre: K-Pop, a South Korean music genre, has gained worldwide popularity with groups like BTS, BLACKPINK, and EXO, known for their dance style, fashion, and visual production.

Beethoven's Piano: Ludwig van Beethoven continued composing music even after losing his hearing. To communicate with others, he used a piano and wrote notes.

The Mozart Effect: The "Mozart effect" suggests that exposure to Mozart's music may have temporary benefits on cognitive functions, although the original claim has been questioned.

The Infamously Notorious Chord: The three-note triad chord "diabolus in musica" (devil in music), also known as the devil's chord, is considered dissonant and has been avoided in certain musical eras and contexts.

The First Music Video: "Video Killed the Radio Star" by The Buggles was the first music video aired on MTV on August 1, 1981, marking the beginning of the era of music videos.

Slash's Famous Guitar: Slash, the guitarist of Guns N' Roses, is known for his iconic Les Paul guitar and his solo in "Sweet Child o' Mine."

Music and Therapy: Music therapy is used as a form of treatment in mental and physical health fields, using music to enhance well-being and address various medical conditions.

The First Vinyl Record: The first vinyl record was created by Emil Berliner in 1889 and, despite technological advances, is still used today by analog music enthusiasts.

Piano at the Age of Three: Wolfgang Amadeus Mozart began playing the piano at the age of three and composed his first symphony at the age of eight.

The "Gangnam Style" Phenomenon: PSY's "Gangnam Style" became a global phenomenon in 2012 and was the first video to reach one billion views on YouTube.

The Wilhelm Scream in Cinema: The Wilhelm Scream, a sound effect used in movies, has become a sort of inside joke in the film industry, appearing in numerous films since the 1950s.

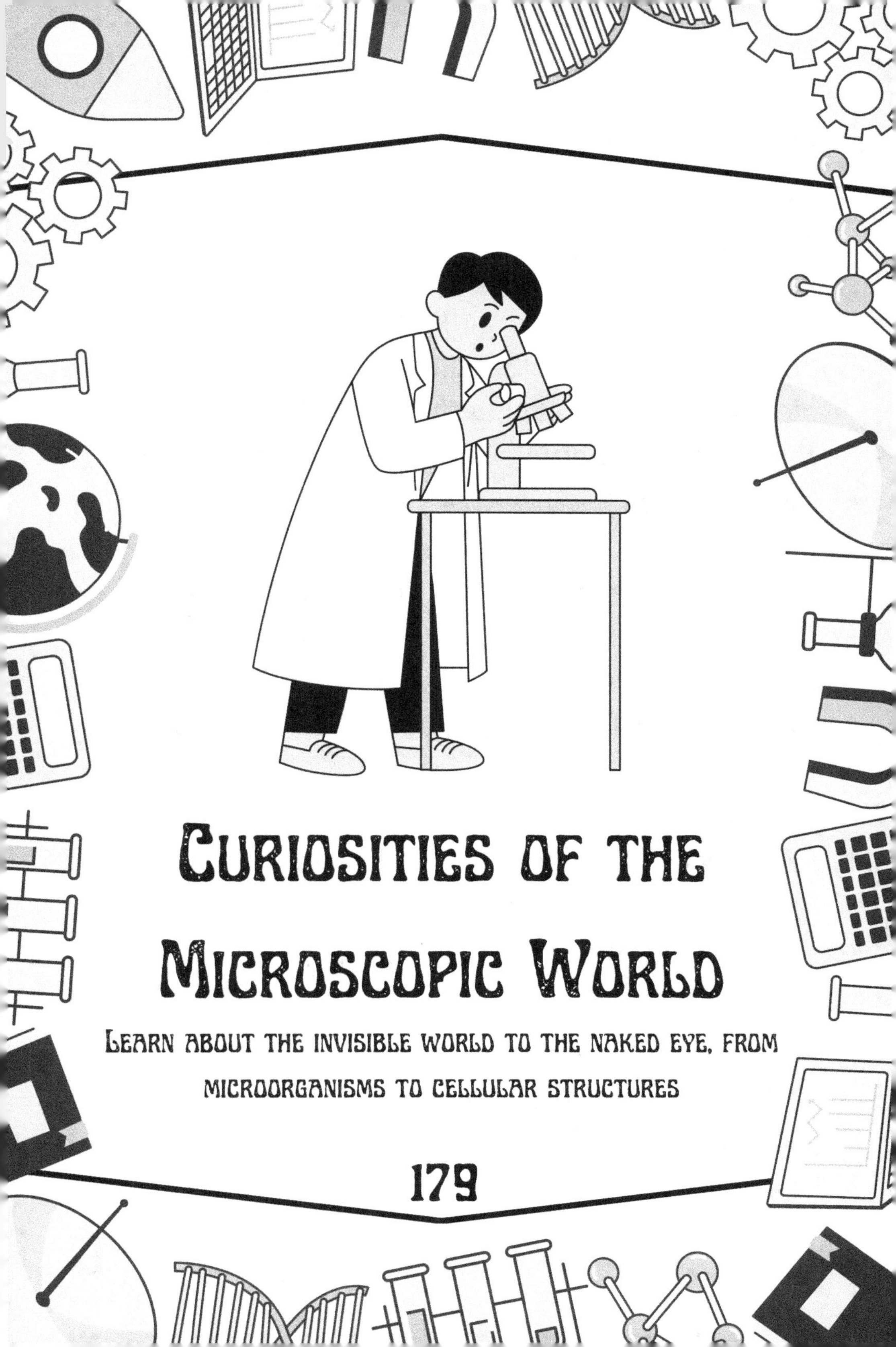

CURIOSITIES OF THE
MICROSCOPIC WORLD
LEARN ABOUT THE INVISIBLE WORLD TO THE NAKED EYE, FROM
MICROORGANISMS TO CELLULAR STRUCTURES
179

Giant Viruses: While many viruses are microscopic, some giant viruses, such as the mimivirus, are large enough to be visible with a standard optical microscope.

Bioluminescent Microorganisms: Some microorganisms, like certain types of plankton, are bioluminescent, meaning they emit their own light. This is especially visible in dark environments, such as the ocean floor.

Microbes in the Human Body: The human body hosts a large number of microorganisms, including bacteria, fungi, and viruses, outnumbering human cells at a ratio of approximately 10 to 1.

Soil Microfauna: The soil contains an astonishing diversity of microorganisms, such as nematodes and protozoa, playing a crucial role in the decomposition of organic matter and soil formation.

Bacteria in Clouds: Storm clouds can harbor bacteria that act as condensation nuclei, contributing to the process of raindrop formation.

Life in Dew Drops: In humid environments, dew drops can harbor microorganisms, creating temporary microecosystems where these organisms can thrive.

Protozoa in Water: Freshwater and bodies of water are filled with protozoa, single-celled microorganisms that are a fundamental part of the aquatic food chain.

Extremeophile Microorganisms: Some microorganisms, known as extremophiles, can survive in extreme conditions such as high temperatures, high pressure, or highly acidic environments.

Microbes in Glaciers: Even in glaciers, microbial communities have been discovered that can survive in conditions of extreme cold and low nutrient availability.

Biodegrading Microorganisms: Many microorganisms play an essential role in the decomposition of organic matter, contributing to the recycling of nutrients in ecosystems.

The Global Mycelial Network: Fungi form microscopic networks of filaments called mycelia, which can spread over vast areas of soil, connecting plants and facilitating the exchange of nutrients.

Microbial Fermentation: Fermentation, a microbial process, is used in the production of foods such as bread, beer, and yogurt, where microorganisms break down compounds to produce useful end products.

Bacteria in the Ocean: Phytoplankton, primarily composed of bacteria and microscopic algae, produces the majority of Earth's oxygen through photosynthesis in the oceans.

Bioluminescent Microorganisms on Land: In addition to marine organisms, some bioluminescent fungi and worms are also found in terrestrial environments, creating flashes of light in the darkness.

Endosymbiotic Organisms: Some eukaryotic cells contain microorganisms in symbiosis, such as mitochondria, believed to have a bacterial origin.

World of Viruses: Although viruses are not considered cells, they are microscopic entities that infect cells and can have diverse shapes, ranging from spherical to helical.

Mycorrhizal Fungi: Mycorrhizal fungi establish symbiosis with plant roots, assisting them in absorbing nutrients from the soil in exchange for organic compounds.

Cyanobacteria and Oxygen: Cyanobacteria, formerly known as blue-green algae, were responsible for releasing oxygen into the Earth's early atmosphere through photosynthesis.

Bacteriophages: Bacteriophages are viruses that infect bacteria, playing a crucial role in regulating bacterial populations in various environments.

Cellular Structures: Cells, the fundamental units of life, contain various structures such as the nucleus, mitochondria, and endoplasmic reticulum, each performing specific functions to sustain cellular life.

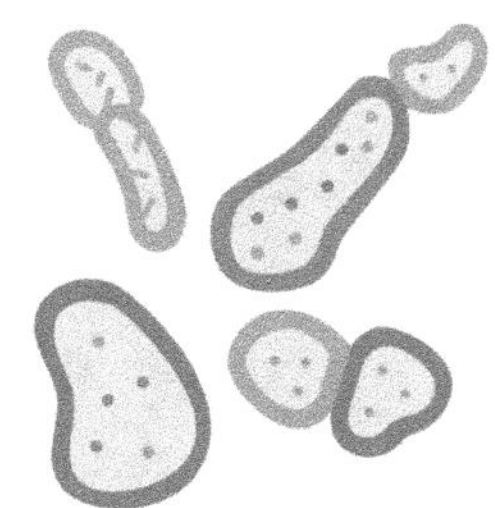

NEW YEAR TRADITIONS AROUND THE WORLD

DISCOVER UNIQUE WAYS IN WHICH DIFFERENT CULTURES CELEBRATE THE ARRIVAL OF THE NEW YEAR

Burning of Dolls in Ecuador: In Ecuador, people burn dolls called "años viejos" to bid farewell to the departing year and welcome the new one.

Kite Flying in Japan: In Japan, people often fly kites on the first day of the year to ward off evil spirits and attract good fortune.

Fireworks in Sydney: Sydney, Australia, is famous for its spectacular fireworks in Sydney Harbour to welcome the New Year.

Wishing Lanterns in Thailand: In Thailand, releasing illuminated paper lanterns, known as "khom loi," is a tradition to wish for good luck and ward off misfortune.

The 12 Grapes of Spain: In Spain, it is traditional to eat 12 grapes at midnight, representing the last 12 seconds of the year, to attract good luck for each month of the upcoming year.

185

Cold-Water Swim in the Netherlands: Some people in the Netherlands participate in the "Nieuwjaarsduik," a cold-water swim on January 1st as a brave and refreshing act to start the new year.

House Cleaning Ritual in China: Before the Chinese New Year, it is common to thoroughly clean homes to sweep away accumulated bad luck from the ending year.

Fortune Cookies in the United States: On New Year's Eve, many people in the United States enjoy fortune cookies containing positive and sometimes humorous messages.

108 Bell Ceremony in Japan: In Japan, some temples perform the "Joya no Kane," a ceremony of 108 tolls to ward off the 108 worldly desires and purify the soul.

Placing Money in Shoes in Greece: In Greece, it is customary to place money in shoes on New Year's Eve to attract prosperity and good fortune.

Visit to Cemeteries in Mexico: In Mexico, some people visit cemeteries to remember their departed loved ones and pay tribute to them during the transition to the new year.

Throwing Old Items in Italy: In some regions of Italy, people throw old objects out of the window on New Year's Eve as a symbolic gesture of leaving the past behind and welcoming the new.

Building Snowmen in Russia: In Russia, building snowmen is a popular activity during New Year celebrations, especially in snow-covered areas.

Burning Wishes in Scotland: In Scotland, the Hogmanay, the New Year celebration, often includes the burning of barrels and writing wishes on pieces of paper that are then set on fire.

Eating Lentil Soup in Italy: In Italy, eating lentil soup on New Year's Eve is considered a symbol of prosperity and good fortune due to the shape of lentils resembling coins.

Duck Parade in South Korea: In South Korea, the duck parade on New Year's Eve symbolizes prosperity and good luck.

Jumping from Chairs in Denmark: In Denmark, it is a tradition to jump from chairs at midnight to "leap" into the new year and leave bad luck behind.

Gifting Gingerbread in Sweden: In Sweden, it is common to give gingerbread with positive messages during New Year celebrations.

Wearing Colored Underwear in Latin America: In many Latin American cultures, wearing specific colored underwear on New Year's Eve is associated with different wishes and purposes for the upcoming year.

Sweeping the House in Puerto Rico: In Puerto Rico, sweeping the house outward symbolizes getting rid of the bad luck and negativity from the previous year.

188

Thank you!

If you enjoyed this book, you can leave me a comment in the Amazon reviews; I would be very grateful, and it will be of great help for my upcoming publications.

How can I make you happy in my next book?

See
you!

www.ingramcontent.com/pod-product-compliance
Lightning Source LLC
Chambersburg PA
CBHW050725260726